Management and Control of Currency and Interest Rate Risk

Management and Control of Currency and Interest Rate Risk

BARRY HOWCROFT and
CHRISTOPHER STOREY

PROBUS PUBLISHING COMPANY
Chicago, Illinois

This publication is designed to provide accurate and authoritative information in regard to the subject matter covered. It is sold with the understanding that the publisher is not engaged in rendering legal, accounting or other professional service.

FROM A DECLARATION OF PRINCIPLES JOINTLY ADOPTED BY A COMMITTEE OF THE AMERICAN BAR ASSOCIATION AND A COMMITTEE OF PUBLISHERS.

Library of Congress Cataloging-in-Publication Data

Howcroft, Barry.
    Management and control of currency and interest rate risk.

        1. Hedging (Finance)   2. Financial futures.   3. Options (Finance)   I. Storey, Christopher.   II. Title.
    H06024.A3H68   1989   332.64'5   89-10670

ISBN 1-55738-098-8

Printed in the United States of America

1   2   3   4   5   6   7   8   9   0

Contents

Contents

Contents

Contents

Preface

The past decade has witnessed an unprecedented era of worldwide currency and interest rate volatility, which has given rise to an equally unprecedented rate of innovation in financial instruments designed to facilitate management in controlling risk and minimising the effect of uncertain cash flows. This book has accordingly been written to provide an introduction to these financial instruments and to develop an understanding of their application, their subsequent development and relative merits.

The book will be useful to those operating in a wide variety of organisations including banks, securities houses, foreign exchange brokers, dealers, etc. and treasurers in the corporate sector. Ideally, the reader will be familiar with basic economic theory but there is no prerequisite for a knowledge of the fundamentals of exposure management.

Essentially, our intention has been to write a book that concentrates upon the instruments and principles of hedging. As such we commence with the 'forefather' of modern hedging techniques, namely, forward exchange, and then develop the notion of forward options. Second and third generation hedging instruments and principles are then discussed and include: currency options, traded currency options, break forward contracts, currency futures, interest rate futures, interest rate options, forward rate agreements, gilt futures, US treasury bond futures and swaps.

Finally, may we thank everybody who has contributed either directly or indirectly to the writing of the book, particularly for their patience and understanding.

Barry Howcroft
Christopher Storey

Introduction

From 1945 until the early 1970s there was relatively little volatility in either exchange rates or interest rates. Commensurately little time was, therefore, devoted to either currency risk or interest rate risk management. Currency stability had been virtually assured by the Bretton Woods agreement of 1945, which effectively fixed exchange rates to a par value. Exchange fluctuations were, therefore, usually both small and predictable. Interest rate stability was similarly assured, as it was actively pursued by westernised governments as a major economic objective, under the post-war Keynesian era.

Catalysts of Volatility

By modern day standards the pre-early 1970s financial managers had a correspondingly straightforward, almost simplistic function. Basically they concentrated upon credit considerations that typically related to yield/cost versus liquidity, rather than the active management of risk. However, during the course of the 1970s several related events occurred that had significant effects on the international economy and the function of financial markets. The events in question were as follows:

1. The introduction of floating exchange rates which replaced the Bretton Woods system of fixed exchange rates.
2. The oil price crisis and the introduction of monetarist economic policies by most westernised economies to replace the Keynesian policies that had prevailed since 1945.

Floating Exchange Rates

The Smithsonian agreement of 1971 increased the fluctuations allowed under the Bretton Woods agreement from the 1% band around the central exchange rate to $2\frac{1}{4}\%$. However, this small relaxation in what was essentially a fixed exchange rate regime proved to be insufficient and in 1973 a system of floating exchange rates was introduced.

1

Introduction

The subsequent volatility of exchange rates introduced a significant degree of uncertainty in business decision making because the sterling value of receipts and payments denominated in a foreign currency became equally uncertain. This problem was exacerbated by the actions of other players in the foreign exchange markets, whose actions tended to cause large cyclical movements in exchange rates.

The move towards floating exchange rates also had an effect upon interest rate volatility. Interest rates are determined not only by domestic monetary policy but also by the phenomena known as the interest rate parity factor, which claims that interest rates throughout the world should bear a close relationship and tend to be equal when account is taken of exchange rate movements. For example, if sterling was expected to depreciate against the dollar, sterling interest rates would have to exceed dollar interest rates by an amount sufficient to compensate the expected loss from holding sterling.

Oil Price Crisis

Oil prices quintupled in 1974 and then tripled over the period 1979–81. This had a dramatic effect upon the net flows of international savings and investments, with the result that massive amounts of petro dollars, held by the oil exporting nations, moved around the world's financial markets in search of bank deposits offering the highest returns.

Oil importing countries had unprecedented balance of payments deficits. Industrial countries reacted in two ways: firstly, they introduced deflationary policies to reduce domestic demand and secondly, they attracted capital from the oil exporting nations by the inducement of high interest rates and relatively risk free, highly liquid investments. This capital was subsequently used to finance the balance of payments deficits of the developing countries, perhaps best typified by Latin America. This process, referred to as 'recycling', eventually culminated in the international debt crisis of 1982.

Monetarist Policies

The change from Keynesian to monetarist policies resulted in a change in policy targets away from stable interest rates towards the pursuit of intermediate monetary aggregates, which had the effect of increasing volatility. Combined with the removal of interest rate ceilings, this meant that in times of tight monetary policy the price mechanism worked mostly through higher interest rates rather than through the quantity mechanism of tighter available credit.

This change in economic emphasis occurred not only in the United

Kingdom but also in the United States with the adoption by the Federal Reserve of its New Economic Policy in October 1979. To achieve a stable growth in the money supply, interest rates had to be manipulated, thus volatility was shifted from the money supply towards interest rates.

Effects of Volatility

Volatility induced both companies and financial institutions to react in two quite distinct ways to the changing environment. Firstly, they introduced and improved their methods of assessing their immediate environment and, secondly, introduced forecasting techniques to predict and anticipate possible changes. The latter approach to the problem of volatility has had limited success, with the result that emphasis changed from attempting to forecast possible changes towards one of obtaining advance protection against possible future changes. In essence the whole emphasis changed towards management of risk by identifying exposures and using the array of new and emerging financial instruments to reduce the possible harmful effects of volatility.

Players in the Market

The financial markets consist of many players who perform distinct roles and who can be categorised according to whether they are trading, hedging or speculating.

Trading is a generic term for all market participants and can, in a general sense, be defined as the commercial users and suppliers of the market. In the United States, the term has a different meaning and is typically used to denote a market player who is speculating. Conversely, hedging is a specific term for a market participant who attempts to cover perceived risk exposure. Hedging risk, therefore, is synonymous with transferring risk and is directly concerned with ensuring that losses from adverse movements in either interest rates or exchange rates are compensated by offsetting gains from the hedge.

Speculators are effectively the opposite of hedgers as they trade in the anticipation of profiting from subsequent price movements. They are prepared to assume the capital risk associated with maintaining an exposed position and, as such, are the risk takers within the market.

Both hedgers and speculators are necessary for the efficient working of any financial market. Speculators provide the necessary liquidity by bridging the gaps in the market between demand and supply, thereby allowing hedgers to buy or sell in sufficient volumes without much difficulty.

3

CHAPTER 1

Forward exchange

1.1 Introduction

The forward rate for a currency is the price at which the currency can be bought (or sold) for delivery at a future date. There are a number of risks attached to forward dealing which make it essential to exercise greater care than for a spot transaction. For instance, the forward rate is not purely a reflection of the strength or weakness of a currency, it also allows for interest rate differentials, and thus forward rates may move even more dramatically than spot rates. Conversely, the ability to cover risks in the forward markets makes it easier for corporate treasurers to ascertain the future value of assets and liabilities.

1.2 Forward Margins

Forward margins are calculated from the interest differentials that exist between two currencies and the duration of the contract. The margin is then either added or subtracted from the spot rate depending upon whether the currency is at a premium or discount. Example 1.1 will help to clarify this point.

Example 1.1 Calculating forward exchange rates

Suppose a market making bank quotes spot UK pounds–US dollars (GBP–USD) at $1.5999–01. In the United Kingdom, interest rates are 9% per annum while in the United States the equivalent interest rates are about 8%, a 1% per annum differential. In the three month period the margin has to be about 1% and since 1% of $1.60 = 0.0160, the three month rate must be somewhere around $0.0160/4 = 0.004. To be really accurate we should have used the arbitrage equation, i.e.:

$$\text{Premium} = \frac{ID \times S \times D}{360 \times 100 \times (D \times RB)}$$

where

ID	=	interest differential
S	=	spot rate
D	=	days forward
RB	=	base currency deposit rate

Note the use of 360 days where the base currency is US dollars. This would have given us a three month forward exchange rate of 0.00394.

Whereas £1 can be sold for $1.5999 on the spot, only $1.5758 will be received for £1 delivered in one month's time. Because of the interest differential forward dollars are at a premium (i.e. sterling at a discount). In other words, more sterling will have to be paid to obtain the same amount of dollars for delivery in three months' time, than would be the case for an equivalent amount of dollars on the spot.

Suppose the dollar was at a discount (US interest rates > UK interest rates) the forward prices may now look like:

Dollar at a discount

Spot £/$	1.5999–01
3 months £/$	39–41
3 months outright rate	1.6038–1.6042

In this instance the forward margins will be quoted in reverse order (i.e. ascending rather than descending order) and added to the spot price. This must be so as, otherwise, the spread would narrow for far dates, which can never be the case.

1.3 Direct and Indirect Quotations

The rule for forward margins with indirect quotations (amount of foreign currency per one unit of home currency, e.g. £/$ rate) is that when the larger number precedes the smaller number the foreign currency is at a premium and the forward margin has to be deducted from the spot. When the smaller number precedes the larger it is at a discount and the forward margin has to be added to the respective spot rate.

In a situation where a currency is quoted directly, the interpretation is the same. For example, dollar–Deutschmark (given as number of Deutschmarks per dollar):

	Dollar at discount	Dollar at a premium
Spot $/DM	1.8880–85	1.8880–85
3 months $/DM	56–51	51–56
Outright rate	1.8824–34	1.8931–41

Forward exchange

Though the quotations are direct, the principle remains the same – fewer Deutschmarks will have to be expended in the forward market to buy the same amount of dollars. Therefore, forward Deutschmarks are at a premium, whereas in the second set of figures the Deutschmark is at a discount as more Deutschmarks will have to be paid to buy forward dollars.

1.4 Premiums and Discounts

Discounts in direct quotations involve higher interest rates for the currency which is valued in the home currency, e.g. where the dollar is at a discount against the Deutschmark, the forward margin as quoted in Frankfurt will be deducted. This means that effective interest rates for dollars must be higher than those for Deutschmarks. On the other hand, premiums would show that higher yields are obtainable for Deutschmarks than for dollars. It should be pointed out that when the dollar is at a discount in Frankfurt, the Deutschmark is at a premium in New York.

1.5 Importance of the Forward Market

The forward market is of importance to corporate treasurers because they can fix the cost of imports and exports in advance of the time that payments have to be made or receivables converted. Provided the treasurer contracts with a reputable bank his only risk is that of non-receipt of good or non-payment, which will leave him with an exposed currency position. The main users of the forward markets are as follows:

1. Those who invest abroad.
2. Those who borrow abroad.
3. Exporters.
4. Speculators.

They use the forward market to reduce their foreign exchange risk, or exposure. This behaviour is described as hedging or covering and allows the bank's customer to lock into a set rate for a set date in the future. There is therefore no opportunity to take advantage of a favourable rate move. Figure 1.1 below shows the profit/loss (P/L) line for spot and forward transactions.

1.6 Forward Foreign Exchange Swaps

The majority of forward contracts do not exist as outright agreements but, rather, take the forms of swaps. A swap transaction is the simultaneous buying and selling of a foreign currency in approximately equal amounts, for different maturity dates. The most common form of swap is to base the second trade on a forward exchange.

6

Forward foreign exchange swaps

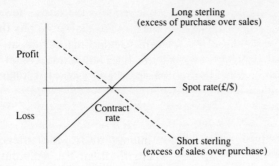

Figure 1.1   Profit and loss line for spot and forward contracts

The most important point to note is that although a swap operation eliminates most of the exchange exposure it still attracts spot rate risk and interest rate differential risk. The only way to avoid this is to sell interest flows forward, or to sell their present value at spot (a spot hedge).

Example 1.2 Pricing currency swaps
Using the preceding example (Example 1.1) we can see how the pricing of a currency swap is arrived at:

Spot £/$	=	1.5999–01
3 months £/$	=	41–39
Outright rate for 3 months	=	1.5958–1.5962
The swap rates for 3 months, then	=	41–39

Outright prices would be used for buying and selling currencies with corporate customers and banks which do not specialise in foreign exchange or in the particular currency in which the market maker operates. The market-makers in forward transactions operate a simultaneous buying and selling approach because this allows them to concentrate on the most important aspect of forward rates, namely, interest differentials.

Swaps are very valuable to those who are investing or borrowing abroad. For example, a person who invests in a foreign treasury bill can include a spot–forward swap to avoid foreign exchange risk. The investor sells forward the maturity value of the bill at the same time as the spot foreign exchange is purchased. Since a known amount of the investor's local currency will be delivered according to the forward contract, no uncertainty from exchange rates is faced. In a similar way, those who borrow in foreign markets can buy forward the foreign currency needed for repayment at the same time as they convert the borrowed foreign funds on the spot market. The value of currency swaps to international investors and borrowers helps to explain their popularity.

1.7 Forward Exchange Risk

The main risks typically associated with a forward exchange contract are the settlement risk and the counterparty risk: the former is concerned with the risk that the customer may not be in a position to honour his part of the contract. This will entail the bank completing the contract at maturity by buying or selling currency on the foreign exchange markets. The risk of loss can be greatly reduced by 'netting contracts' between banks, otherwise the bank's risk will be determined by the rates prevailing at the time of maturity and by the bank's ability to pass the loss onto the customer. The counterparty risk typically gives rise to the settlement risk and is concerned with the risk that the customer will not be able to complete the contract due to failure of the underlying commercial arrangements. This will involve the customer having to close out the contract on maturity at the appropriate spot rate, which will determine the ultimate loss or profit.

In instances where a corporate customer is not in a position to determine the exact arrival or departure dates of imports or exports, it may be beneficial to employ a forward option. Although option contracts can be for distant maturities, the actual option period is usually limited to the shortest possible time span. This is because duration is probably the most important concept in determining interest rate differential risk and, therefore, the eventual forward exchange rate.

1.8 Forward Options (Option Date Forward Contracts)

A forward option (an FX option) gives the customer the opportunity to buy a specific currency at any time between two forward dates (e.g. at any time between five and six months in the future) known as the 'near date' and 'far date'. The length of time between these dates is known as the option period.

1.9 Length of an Option Period

How is an option period decided upon? An importer may have negotiated a contract to import a machine tool from abroad and whether the transaction is covered by a documentary credit or is on an open account basis, it is likely that between the time of negotiation and the actual arrival of the items, between three and six months will have elapsed.

The importer is naturally interested in making sure that the cost of the machine tool will not be higher than the amount he contracted for, but his problem is the uncertainty about the date of payment. Given that the earliest shipment that can be expected is in five months' time (but that it is unlikely to exceed six), the importer can be reasonably certain that payment will have to be made sometime in this period and, whether now or at a later date, the foreign currency will have to be acquired. Knowing the approximate timing he can contact his bank and explain that he would like the bank to quote a buyer's option to run from the five to six month forward date. It is always preferable to buy or sell option periods in dealing months, as prices for these standard periods are usually available for up to one year in the major currencies.

The bank writing the option can either take the view that it is better to cover the exposure by buying or selling early on in the option period or to sell for the last date or the middle of the period, depending upon previous experience with the buyer of the option.

1.10 Pricing a Forward Option

As for all exchange quotations, the option rates are based on the worst possible outcome for the quoting bank and, consequently, the worst rate for the client. Applying the option procedure to a hypothetical import transaction into the United Kingdom, the customer and bank would act as in Example 1.3 below:

Example 1.3 Option pricing (a)

The customer would contact a bank in the City of London and indicate an interest in buying dollars for the five to six month option period. The bank would then either use its own quotations, or check the rates in the market which have a bearing on the option price. The rates the bank obtains are:

Spot £/$	1.5850–55
5 month	66–58
6 month	79–71

Initially, the bank would have to look at the worst possible outcome that could develop. The customer can exercise his option at any time between the five and six months. He might not take up an option until the last day (corresponding with the six month date). Consequently, the dealer would have to compute his rate on the six month quotation and price the option not worse than $1.5850 - 0.0079 = 1.5771$. The dealer would have to base his initial price on the view that, as the customer does not have to take up his option until the six month date, this particular option is identical to a normal outright sale for six months' delivery.

Given that the rates shown above hold good for another client interested in selling dollars for the same option period, then obviously the bank would use the buying spot rate of $1.5855 - 58 = 1.5797$. The dealer would not give the benefit of the six month rate to the customer, as the latter might exercise the option on the first day, i.e. the date corresponding with the standard five

9

month maturity date. The reasoning of the dealer is the reverse of that applied to the buyer's option contract. He hopes that his customer will refrain from exercising the option until the last day open to him. In other words, both for buying and selling options – assuming there is no change in the forward rate structure – the first and the last days, respectively, would seem the optimum days provided the foreign currency (US dollars) is at a premium.

1.11   Option Cover

So far, the customer has covered his FX risk and will obtain payment when necessary. The bank, however, will be subject to the exposure that the option contract has produced. The best way to cover this is the subject of much debate. The purist view is that an option should be covered from the first day the option can be exercised, i.e.:

● where granting a buyer's option obtain cover for the first option day;
● where granting a seller's option, sell for the first option day.

In principle, everything would be fine if the beneficiary of an option did exactly that, but in practice this is not always the case. The more adventurous approach is to match the exposure by buying or selling for the last option date. This approach assumes that, whatever happens, a customer will not call his option until the last day and that the market-maker is in a position to forecast the forwards at some time in the future. Both extremes carry risks and are contrary to the philosophy that all dealing risks should be brought back to an acceptable level. In practice, a compromise is sought and a five to six month option, whether buying or selling, is usually covered somewhere in the middle. For relatively short options of up to six months, the dealer usually has a fairly good idea of what the forward rates should be as the maturity of the deal grows closer, or at the very least will know whether they will be at a premium or discount.

1.12   Effect of Premiums and Discounts

It is interesting to look at the dealer's approach when the US dollar is at a discount against sterling, as in the following schedule (interest rate difference $= 1.5\%$):

Example 1.4   Option pricing (b)

Spot rate	1.6010–1.6015
5 months	100–100
6 months	120–130

Effect of premiums and discounts

If the buyer of a five against six month option (i.e. buying £ now) went to his banker, he would get a different interpretation. Instead of being charged the six month rate, the dealer would apply the five month rate, thus:

$$1.6010 + 100 = 1.6110$$

The buyer most certainly would not get the benefit of the longer maturity. As the dollar is at a discount, it is no longer of advantage to the dealer to have the buyer exercise his option on the first day, rather, the last day is now the optimum day for the writer. If the buyer took up his option on the first day, the market-maker would have to enter the market to buy dollars for the option date against any forward date he had originally chosen to cover the exposure.

Where a currency is at a premium in the forwards and is expected to remain so, it is advisable, for a buyer's option, to take the cover no earlier than the middle date of the option period. The worst that can happen is that the buyer takes delivery on the last possible day. Conversely, subject to previous experience, a seller's option should be sold for delivery not later than the middle of the option period.

The magnitude of anticipated forward levels has a bearing on the decision whether to cover early or late during the option period. In many active dealing banks, it is not even standard practice to cover option contracts unless they are for substantial amounts or for very long maturities.

Returning to our preceding example of a buyer of a five against a six month option on the £/$. An ultra-conservative attitude would encourage covering the exposure by buying sterling for the first option date (five months); the probability of the option being called on the first day is negligible and cover taken out for the middle of the period would limit the risk of the position having to be unwound for a whole month.

The posturing of the market-makers to limit an option exposure risk can be summarised as in Table 1.1.

The summary assumes that there will be little change in the forward structure and that the relationship of the interest rates for the two currencies will remain at the existing equilibrium. Nevertheless, the giver of the option will try to protect himself from what he considers to be the worst possible outcome. To overcome the problem of deciding which currencies are at a premium or discount in the above schedule, we must assume that the currency which is being priced, in terms of another one, is being sold or bought.

For long term options, six months or longer, especially when the amounts involved are substantial, it would be safer still to take out the

Forward exchange

Table 1.1. Option contract cover schedule

	Rate for buyers' option	Rate for seller's option	Cover date
Forward premium	Last day		Middle of period or later
Forward premium		First day	Middle of period or earlier
Forward discount	First day		Middle of period or earlier
Forward discount		Last day	Middle of period or later

cover, spread over the period of the option. A wholesale covering operation for one maturity would leave the option writer too exposed to the vagaries of the market. Furthermore, large option contracts and their cover should be monitored all the time and the maturity structure adjusted to reflect market events or trends.

1.13 Conclusions

Option dealing, while providing greater security to the beneficiary, can also be a profitable venture for the dealer if the positions are created with some forethought. Unfortunately, the liberalisation of the market makes it far more difficult for professional dealers to gain extra profits on forward options as large national and multinational companies, e.g. British Petroleum, are staffed by traders who know the markets just as well as their counterparts in the banks. Accordingly, the question of covering the risk is of great importance to the market-making bank. A much more complicated option, of great significance to risk management, is the currency option which is explained in the next chapter.

CHAPTER 2

Currency options

2.1 Introduction

The currency option involves elements of both hedging and position taking, as it enables a currency transactor to limit downside risk on a currency transaction, while retaining profit potential from a favourable movement in exchange rates.

This chapter concentrates mainly on the technical aspects of over-the-counter (OTC) currency options. Their flexibility compared to the relatively cheaper but standardised traded options makes them highly attractive to corporations. Banks typically design OTCs to satisfy the specific needs of the corporate customers in terms of amount, expiration date and strike price. Not unusually, however, banks themselves will offset OTC options by using traded options.

2.2 Definition

Strictly speaking, currency options are true options as they provide the holder with the right to decide whether to exchange or not. Option date forward contracts, as discussed in Chapter 1, merely provide an option as to the date when exchange will take place but they always require exchange to take place at some time during the option.

Specifically, a currency option gives the holder the right, but not the obligation, to buy or sell the currency on or before a future date, at a specified price in return for a premium. There are two types of option which may be bought or sold – a put option and a call option.

1. A put option gives the holder (the buyer) the right to sell the underlying currency to the writer (seller) of the option, who stands prepared to buy the currency at the option buyer's discretion.
2. The holder of a call option has the right to buy the currency and the writer of the call stands prepared to sell the currency to the holder, at the holder's discretion. To write a call, therefore, is the same as buying a put option and, vice-versa, to write a put is the same as selling a call option, insofar as your currency position is concerned.

2.3 Strike Price

The strike price is the rate at which the option is priced. Exercise of the option will allow the buyer to buy or sell the specified currency at the strike price. An option is referred to as being 'in-the-money', 'out-of-the-money', or 'at-the-money' depending on whether the spot rate is higher, lower or at the strike price.

For example, a strike price of an option to buy Australian dollars (AUD) at a rate of US dollars (USD) 0.68 when the current spot 0.66 is 'out-of-the-money', as it would be cheaper to buy the AUD at USD 0.66 in the spot market rather than exercise the option and pay USD 0.68. However, at a strike price of USD 0.68 with a spot of 0.66, a put on AUD (the right to sell AUD) will be 'in-the-money', as the option could be exercised at USD 0.68 and the USD received then sold in the spot market at USD 0.66 to realise a profit.

2.4 Premium

The premium is the cost to the buyer of obtaining the right to buy or sell the currency and the compensation to the seller for writing that risk over the option period. The premium is paid up-front two business days after the contract is agreed and is expressed as a percentage of the strike price.

The premium for an option will vary according to the style of the option. The two styles for over-the-counter (OTC) options are American and European. An OA (over-American) option may be exercised at any time during the option period and as such commands a larger premium than an OE (over-European) option which may only be exercised on the expiry date.

Exchange traded options (i.e. options traded, for example, on the Philadelphia Stock Exchange, the International Monetary Market in Chicago, the London International Financial Futures Exchange, etc.) are restricted to an American-style option. Exercise or expiry will be determined by the terms of the contract with a typical Philadelphian Stock Exchange option, for example, expiring on the Friday before the third Wednesday in the contract month.

The two key components of an option premium are the intrinsic value and the time value of the contract. These are explained below:

2.5 Intrinsic Value

This is the profit that could be realised if the option were to be exercised immediately after buying it. With a call option it is the excess of the spot price over the strike price. Under such circumstances the option is said to be 'in-the-money' and the holder could profit by exercising the option thereby buying currency relatively cheaply and simultaneously selling it at a higher price. Conversely, when the strike price of a call option is above spot it has no intrinsic value and is said to be 'out-of-the-money'.

With a put option, this is said to be 'in-the-money' when the strike price is in excess of spot. A holder could then realise an immediate profit by purchasing currency cheaply on the spot market and selling it at a higher rate by means of exercising his option. When the put option is 'out-of-the-money', the strike price will be less than spot and the option will have no intrinsic value.

The degree by which the intrinsic value affects the premium is called the delta (this is dealt with later in the chapter).

2.6 Time Value

Time value is the difference between an option's premium and its intrinsic value. As such, time value, which cannot be negative, is a measure of the amount the exchange rate might be expected to move in the buyer's favour during the lifetime of the option.

The overall premium (price) of an option is therefore the sum of its intrinsic value and its time value. Figures 2.1 and 2.2 show the value of put and call options sub-divided into intrinsic value and time value. Time value is represented by the shaded areas and intrinsic value by the 45° line XY.

With call options (Figure 2.1) there is no intrinsic value when spot prices fall below the strike price X. This explains why the intrinsic value line XY commences at this point. When spot prices are above the strike price the increase in intrinsic value will mirror the increases in spot giving rise to a 45° line depicted by XY. The backward slope of the XY line (Figure 2.2)

Figure 2.1   Call option premium

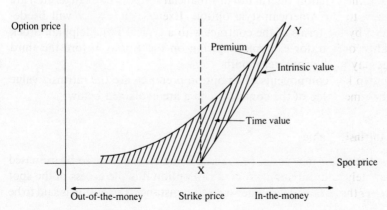

Currency options

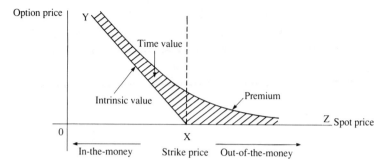

Figure 2.2 Put option premium

shows that with a put option when spot prices are below the strike price the holder can buy foreign currency at a lower price than he can sell it.

When the strike price is equal to the spot price the option is said to be 'at-the-money', and Figures 2.1 and 2.2 both depict clearly that time value is at its greatest at this point. As the option moves either 'in-to-' or 'out-of-money', time value diminishes as indicated by the tendency of option premium curves to approach the intrinsic value boundary OXY (Figure 2.1) and YXZ (Figure 2.2) as the spot price moves further away from the strike price.

The values to the holder of both a put and call option at expiry are shown in Figures 2.3 and 2.4. In the examples the holder can either put (sell) Australian dollars to the writer in exchange for US dollars or call (buy) Australian dollars in exchange for US dollars. A strike price of 0.65 has been assumed along with a premium of 0.02.

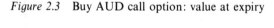

Figure 2.3 Buy AUD call option: value at expiry

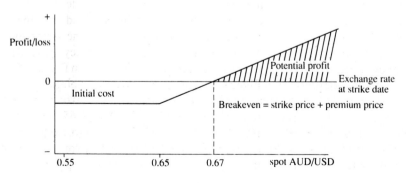

16

Geometry of currency options and forward exchange

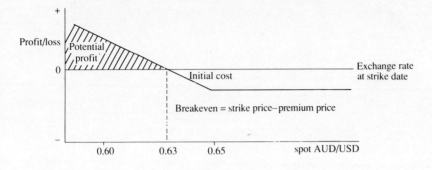

Figure 2.4 Buy AUD put option: value at expiry

As the holder of an option has the right but not the obligation to take up his option, the value of his position can never be negative. He therefore has the means to create an asset or a liability with unlimited upside potential while restricting his downside to the difference between the forward rate and the price paid for the option.

The real breakeven point for the holder of the option is therefore at a level which covers the future value of the premium originally paid for the option – in our example, 0.67 for the holder of a call option and 0.63 for the holder of a put option. In the case of the writer there is unlimited downside potential. Upside potential is limited to the future value of the premium received. The breakeven point will again be a few points away from the strike price because of the future value of the premium already received.

2.7 Geometry of Currency Options and Forward Exchange

An option position can be adjusted through the use of forward exchange contracts. For example, a speculator who is bullish on the dollar may buy a put on currency. If at a later date the dollar rallies considerably, the speculator may seek to lock in profits. This could be achieved by either selling the put option or, if the speculator is now negative on the dollar, by converting the put into a call through a forward (buy currency forward) exchange contract. The geometry of this relationship is shown in Figure 2.5. The put and call positions in Figures 2.3 and 2.4 have been combined with a forward contract. The graphs are based on a forward sale at 0.65 and the strike prices on both the put and the call options are similarly 0.65. At a rate of 0.6, the loss on the call, po, plus the profit from the forward, xo, is equal to the profit on the put, yo. Similarly, at a rate of 0.7, the profit from the call, yo, less the loss on the forward zo, is equal to the loss, po, on the put option.

Currency options

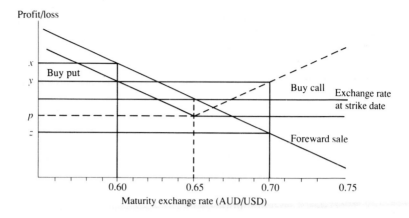

Figure 2.5   Geometry of currency options and forward exchange

2.8   Option Pricing

We have already established that an options premium (or price) consists of two main components, namely, its intrinsic value and its time value. Both these components are particularly affected by the expected volatility of the currency over the duration of the option. Indeed, the main determinants of price can be summarised as follows:

- maturity date;
- today's spot market rate;
- forward rates;
- strike price;
- exercise feature, i.e. European or American;
- interest rate differential of the currencies involved;
- volatility.

2.9   The Maturity Date

This is important because the time value of an option is greater when there is a longer period before the expiration date. This is due to the fact that a longer maturity introduces a much greater possibility of large spot price movements. Usually the first two months of an option period are the most expensive as the price increases steeply over this period. As a result it is proportionally cheaper to buy longer dated options. This is illustrated in Figure 2.6.

In the early days of an option, time value falls fairly slowly but the rate of decay increases as the expiration date draws near. This accelerating decline

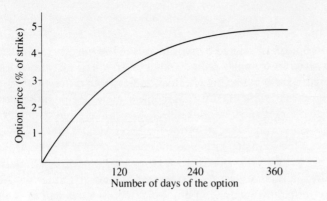

Figure 2.6 Option price versus duration

is entirely consistent with the above statement that time value is greater for options having longer periods to expiration. Time value is, in fact, proportional to the square root of the length of time remaining to expiry date. In effect, when 100 days remain to expiry, time value will be twice that which exists when 25 days remain. Time value will decline by as much during the last 25 days, as it does during the first 75 days. Figure 2.7 shows the accelerating decay of time value for three and six month options.

The curve for the six months' contract declines relatively slowly over the first four months. A long options position in this period would cost little to run on a time value basis, given no movement in the spot price. Over the last two months this cost would rise alarmingly and a short options position would be profitable. As expected, the initial fall in time value on short dated options is greater than that for longer dated options.

Figure 2.7 Time value decay

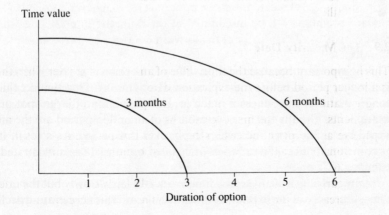

2.10   Interest Rate Differentials

The price of an option is affected by movements in the interest rates of the currencies involved in so much as they influence spot and forward prices. Forward margins are dictated by effective interest rate differentials. For most currencies these differentials are based upon international rather than domestic money market rates. An increase in Australian interest rates, for instance, would tend to push up call option prices on AUD–USD contracts. Conversely, a rise in US interest rates would tend to push call prices down and increase put prices. This is because holding a call option and holding the currency are alternative ways for an investor to take advantage of a rise in the currency price. An increase in domestic interest rates will raise the cost of carry on the underlying currency (the cost of carry is the difference between domestic and foreign interest rates), and will also increase the forward rate. This will make a call option on sterling more attractive and therefore push its price higher. Similarly, a call option on sterling becomes cheaper if foreign interest rates rise. This reduces the cost of carry and the forward price which results in a lower price for the call option.

If the spot price falls, however, but the forward rate remains unchanged by an increase in domestic interest rates, a call option will become cheaper. The downward movement in the spot price will more than offset the increase in the cost of carry, and will push down the price of the call option. In the case of put options, the effect of interest rate movements on the premium will be exactly the opposite of the effect on calls.

2.11   Calculating a Fair Price

The fair price of an option is the premium it should cost in an efficient market. To ascertain the fair price, the minimum price of the option should be calculated. This will be the discounted value of the forward premium for the period, with respect to the strike price or zero, whichever is greater. (The forward premium will be discounted at the domestic interest rate which corresponds to the maturity of the forward contract, i.e. three months, six months, etc.)

If the market price of the option differs from this value there will be an opportunity for making profits from valuation trading. This would involve buying when the market price of the contract is less than the fair price and selling when the market price moved up in line. Conversely, the trader would be selling a contract when the market price is in excess of the fair price in anticipation of the market price subsequently falling in line with the estimated fair price.

Figure 2.8 illustrates the minimum price of a call option on sterling against the US dollar. In this example, UK interest rates are lower than US

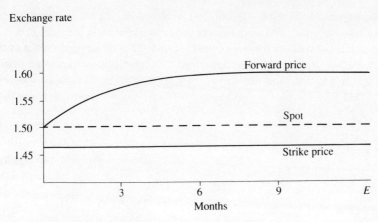

Figure 2.8   Minimum price of a call option: dollar at a discount

rates, and thus forward prices of sterling are higher than the spot price. (The US dollar is at a discount in the forward market.) The minimum price of the call option is the foreword ($1.60) minus the strike price ($1.48) = $0.12, while the intrinsic value is spot ($1.50) minus the strike price ($1.48) = $0.02. If the price of the option were only equal to its intrinsic value, the option could be exercised and sterling sold in the forward market at $1.60 giving an arbitrage valuation profit of $0.10 for each pound.

Figure 2.9 shows the example where UK interest rates are higher than US rates, therefore forward rates are lower than spot rate. The minimum price is equal to the intrinsic value of the call option as the spot price is higher than any of the forward rates. If, however, the strike price were higher than both the spot and forward rates, the minimum price of the option would be zero as the call option would have no intrinsic value.

Figure 2.9   Minimum price of a call option: dollar at a premium

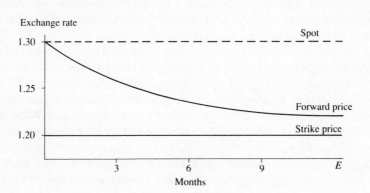

Currency options

The minimum price of a call option is, therefore, the forward minus the strike price or spot minus the strike price, whichever is greater. For put options it is the strike price minus the forward or the strike price minus spot, whichever is greater. The fundamental currency option boundary conditions for a call option are shown in Figure 2.10.

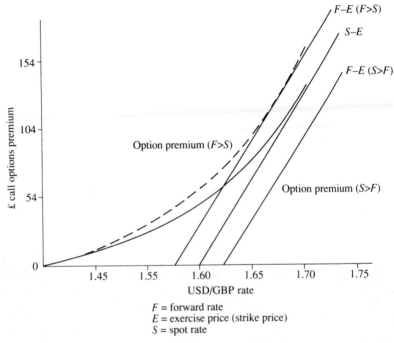

Figure 2.10 Currency option boundary conditions on a call option

2.12 Volatility

Volatility is probably the most important factor in option pricing. A trader who anticipates increased expectation of market volatility can buy options and subsequently sell them at a profit when such anticipation becomes a reality. This increase in the potential to exercise options profitably not only increases the option buyer's willingness to pay higher premiums but simultaneously affords the option writer with the justification to acquire higher premiums.

When applied to options, volatility is typically defined as an annualised statistical measure of the day-to-day fluctuation in the underlying currency price. The statistical measure is the standard deviation where the rule of thumb is that a price may be expected to stay within plus or minus one standard deviation of its current level approximately 67% of the time, and within two standard deviations 95% of the time (Figure 2.11).

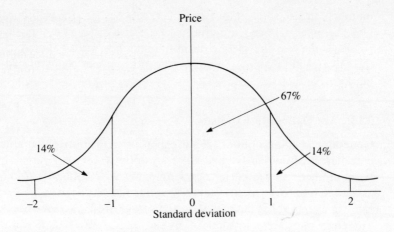

Figure 2.11 Normal distribution of currency rate over time

Suppose the volatility of sterling against the dollar is 0.75%. As the convention in options is to annualise volatility this figure is multiplied by the square root of the number of trading days in a year – approximately 250. So annualised volatility is equal to

$$0.75\% \times \sqrt{250} \simeq 12\% \ (11.8\%)$$

Volatility is both uncertain and highly subjective. Not unusually, traders will be working with slightly different volatility figures for the same currency. Typically, traders will ascertain 'implied volatility' from the market itself by obtaining the market price for an option and contrasting it with the strike price and underlying price. Account must also be taken of the time to maturity and the risk free interest.

Despite the problems in ascertaining volatility it is, nevertheless, an important determinant of price, being an integral factor in mathematical models used for calculating the theoretical price of options. The first of these models was devised by Professors Fisher Black and Myron Scholes in 1973. Utilising standard deviation and probability theory, it attempted to determine whether the option premium covered a probable price change in a stock price over a given period.

The commonly accepted definitive pricing model for foreign exchange options today is a development of the Black–Scholes model. Devised and published by Professors Garman and Kohlhagen in 1983, it refines the earlier model by making an allowance for the interest rate differentials that exist between two currencies involved in an option. However, like most statistical models it assumes a perfect market when in reality the foreign exchange market is far from perfect (see Appendix 1).

Small changes in the estimation of volatility (an integral factor in the

23

models) can also account for large differences between the theoretical price and the market price. In addition to a feel for the situation, therefore, prudence dictates that before quoting premiums writers should calculate the theoretical price and compare it to other prices being quoted in the market.

2.13   Are Options to Expensive?

Generally speaking, options are still expensive in relation to the value of the currency involved. On average, currency options cost approximately 6% a year on major traded currencies. Compared with annual fluctuations in exchange rates over recent years 6% seems reasonable. The £/$ exchange rate, for example, has fluctuated by an average of 13% a year since floating exchange rates were introduced in the early 1970s. Moreover, unlike forwards and futures, downside risk is strictly limited to a known amount while the ability to speculate on the upside potential of currency movements is unlimited.

CHAPTER 3

Hedging using options

3.1 Introduction

Hedging is a management technique aimed at reducing exposure as distinct from speculation, which is the increasing of potential profit. Hedging strategies can be categorised as follows: hedge nothing, hedge everything, or hedge selectively. The use of options in hedging introduces a good deal of flexibility into risk management as the following example shows:

Example 3.1

Suppose customer ABC has US dollar receivables in three months' time, the company's expenses are in Deutschmarks (DM). The current spot rate for dollar-mark is 1.85 and the company treasurer has decided to use an option to cover his exposure taking the view that the DM will appreciate against the USD during the three month period. An option for the right to buy DM against USD with a strike price of 1.85 is required – a call on the DM against the US dollar.

The banks quote to write this option is 2% of the DM amount (equivalent to 0.037 in relation to the spot price).

The premium is calculated as being:

DM 20,000 per DM 1,000,000, i.e. (1,000,000 × 2/100).

ABC must pay this premium two business days after the transaction is agreed.

On the expiry date three months later when the company wishes to exchange USD for DM, two situations are possible:

1. If the dollar–Deutschmark is above DM 1.85, the option should be allowed to expire.
2. If the dollar–Deutschmark is below DM 1.85, the company should exercise the option to buy DM at 1.85.

In the case of 1, the DM should be bought in the spot market. Any price above (1.85 + 0.037) = 1.8870 would represent an additional gain to the

Hedging using options

company above the expected receipts from the exchange. In the case of 2, provided the dollar–Deutschmark is lower than USD 1.8130 (1.85 − 0.037) the cost of the option will have been covered.

A further possibility might be that during the three month period the dollar–Deutschmark has fallen to 1.75. In the event that company ABC thought this rate overvalued the DM, the option could be sold back, realising a profit and receiving back any time value remaining in the option. The company would be left with its original exposure but with considerable profits as a cushion against adverse movement.

3.2   Hedge Ratio (the delta)

Option traders are always checking to ascertain whether an option is cheap or expensive in relation to its fair value. Where the spot price moves favourably, the intrinsic value of an option rises by the same amount and this affects the price accordingly. The degree by which it affects the option price is determined by the hedge ratio or delta factor which is the instantaneous rate of change of a currency option in relation to its underlying currency:

$$= \frac{\text{Change in option premium}}{\text{Change in spot price}}$$

Figure 3.1 shows diagrammatically the effect that changes in spot and option premium have on the delta. Spot rate movement on an out-of-the-money option will be small and the delta will be less than 0.5. For an at-the-money option, the effect of a spot price change will be greater and the delta will be approximately 0.5. As the option becomes more in-the-money the delta will approach 1. The delta also indicates the likelihood of the option being exercised: the higher the delta, the more likely it is that the option will

Figure 3.1   The delta ratio

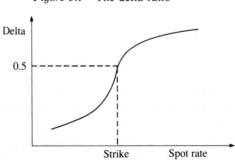

be exercised (see Appendix 2 for an arithmetic calculation of the delta for a currency call option).

If, for example, the dollar price of sterling increased by 1 cent, resulting in a 0.2 cent increase in the premium of a sterling call option, the delta of the option would be 0.2. Thus, with an underlying contract of, say, £1,000,000, a delta of 0.2 implies that an exchange rate rise of 1 cent (worth $10,000 to the underlying contract) would change the value of the option by $2,000. In essence, if spot moved from 1.80 to 1.79, then the value of the underlying contract would change from $1,800,000 to $1,790,000 and the fair value of an option to sell £1,000,000 at 1.75 would change from, say, $68,000 to $70,000. If the option writer decided to maintain his option delta hedged, then he would sell £200,000 at the outset for 1.80 spot value. In other words, he would sell 0.2 of the underlying contract, worth $2,000 on a one cent move in spot.

3.3 The Ratio Hedge

Instead of simply selling out a profitable position there may exist opportunities to sell an alternative option while obtaining a net flat or 'delta neutral' position. To create this position, the trader buys or sells a specific ratioed amount of option contracts so that any change in the underlying currency will not result in a profit or loss on the overall position. To calculate the proper ratio, the trader should divide the delta for the long position by the delta for the short position. This is shown in Example 3.2 using exchange traded contracts.

Example 3.2 Ratio Hedging

Suppose the trader is long 100 AUD–USD March 0.70 puts with a delta of 0.62. He can create a delta neutral position by selling March 0.75 puts which have a delta of 0.69.

$$\frac{0.62}{0.69} = 0.9 \text{ (delta neutral factor)}$$

The trader needs to sell 90 March 0.75 puts (i.e. 100×0.9) to have a delta neutral or net flat position.

Although the delta is a crucial factor in determining the trading strategies of most participants in options, it needs to be continuously monitored. The delta changes in response to variations in exchange rates, expectations of volatility and expiration date of the option. Consequently, delta hedges need to be changed every time the value of the underlying security changes. Moreover, as delta hedging effectively involves chasing the market, in a 'whipsaw' market this will lead to high losses.

27

Table 3.1. Analysis of option P/L and spot position

	(3)	(2)	(1)	0	1	2	3
% spot move	(3)	(2)	(1)	0	1	2	3
Standard deviation	5.8	3.8	1.9	0	1.9	3.8	5.6
Forecast spot	1.5457	1.5607	1.5766	1.5925	1.6084	1.6244	1.6403
Equiv GBP spot position (£)	211,149	150,343	76,092	(1,376)	(82,879)	(166,126)	(250,843)
Change in spot position (£)	60,806	74,252	77,467	0	(81,504)	(83,247)	(84,717)
USD forecast P/L ($)	(5,303)	(1,983)	(683)	219	(595)	(2,584)	(5,542)

Table 3.2. Seven day option P/L analysis

	(3)	(2)	(1)	0	1	2	3
% spot move	(3)	(2)	(1)	0	1	2	3
Standard deviation	(2.2)	(1.4)	(0.7)	0	0.7	1.4	2.2
Forecast spot	1.5447	1.5606	1.5766	1.5925	1.6084	1.6244	1.6403
Equiv GBP spot position (£)	218,314	155,839	79,670	(592)	(85,082)	(171,463)	(257,989)
Change in spot position (£)	62,475	76,169	80,262	0	(84,491)	(86,381)	(86,526)
USD forecast P/L ($)	(4,184)	(822)	639	1,547	731	1,276	(4,438)

3.4 Interaction of the Option and the Delta

The interaction of an option and its delta transaction is best explained by looking at an example. Suppose the bank has written a three month option to buy £1,000,000 at an exercise price of $1.60 (spot 1.5925) and a delta of 0.43. The premium for the option would be $0.025 \times 1,000,000 = \$25,000$ and to remain delta hedged the bank would need to buy £430,000, i.e. $0.43 \times 1,000,000$ at spot.

Table 3.1 shows the effect of subsequent 1% overnight movements in the spot rate. Clearly we are in a short position because if the spot price remains unchanged at 1.5925 we make money through the time value depreciation on the option. As the spot price falls, the call option moves out-of-the-money, leaving us longer and longer on our equivalent sterling spot position. Accordingly, at a spot rate of 1.5607 we should sell £150,343 to remain delta square.

As the option moves out of the money, its intrinsic value will fall, but the forecast P/L is a loss. This is because in the delta transaction we have bought sterling which has now fallen in value producing a loss which exceeds our profit from the fall in value of the option. Conversely, as the spot prices rise, the 1.60 call moves in-the-money and the option rises in value. We become shorter and shorter of sterling in the delta transaction on which we are making a profit. However, the loss from the rise in value of the option outweighs the profit on the delta position giving a forecast loss of $5,542 at 1.6403.

By continually monitoring the situation and constantly hedging and rehedging as the spot market moves, the trader will attempt to make profits on the delta position which, together with the premium, will hopefully offset (outweigh) any loss that may be incurred from the option. If the buyer of an option undertakes the delta transaction, then he will hope that by 'jobbing' his spot position he can recover the premium paid for the option.

The adjustments to the delta hedge transaction are calculated on the binomial theory of the risk free hedge. The binomial model looks at the probability of one or two events happening over a short period of time. From this one forward point a 'tree' of possible spot market paths is constructed by considering the probability of an up movement in the market against a down movement. At every point in this tree the value of the option and the hedge required in the cash market is computed.

Returning to our example, Table 3.2 shows the forecast P/L on the position over a seven day period. These figures show how the fall in time value has affected the P/L figures. A 2% rise in the spot price gives a forecast P/L of $(1,276) which is approximately given by $(2,584) from Table 3.1 plus six days' time value in our favour (6×219) which gives $(1,270). The slight difference lies in the non-linear decline of option time value. It is also

Table 3.3. Volatility sensitivity analysis

% Change in volatility	(1.5)	(1)	(0.5)	0	0.5	1	1.5
Actual volatility	8.5	9	9.5	10	10.5	11	11.5
GBP spot position	11,183	6,561	2,357	(1,496)	(5,108)	(8,446)	(11,544)
Change in spot position (£)	4,622	4,204	3,853	0	(3,612)	(3,338)	(3,098)
USD forecast P/L ($)	4,545	3,033	1,518	0	(1,522)	(3,047)	(4,574)

interesting to note that as the option moves in-the-money the change in the spot position is fairly constant indicating that the delta is rising at a steady rate.

Table 3.3 illustrates the effect of rising and falling volatility on the option position given that the spot remains constant at 1.5925. If volatility remains unchanged at 10%, there will be no P/L. As volatility rises the value of the call sold will increase and, vice-versa, as volatility decreases the value of the call sold will decrease. As volatility rises, the delta will rise (a greater probability of a favourable price move), showing us to be short on our spot position. As volatility falls so will the delta and we become long on our spot position.

3.5 Volatility Risk

Currency options eliminate the volatility risk for the option buyer; however, the option writer should take full responsibility for hedging the volatility risk in return for the premium. When exchange rates are fluctuating sharply (i.e. volatility increasing), it is possible that the option premium could be totally eroded, leaving the writer with a potentially large loss on the option.

If volatility decreases, the cost of hedging the position will also fall and the writer could gain by generating extra profit from his premium (as the option value has now fallen). Figure 3.2 shows the profit and loss profile on short options positions written at 10%, 12% and 15% volatility.

In retrospect, the options hedge is not the most optimum strategy. If the exchange rate falls it would have been better to have done nothing, while if it had risen it would have been better to sell forward. In essence it is a case of sacrificing the best strategy to avoid the worst outcome.

Figure 3.2   Profit and loss profile for a short options position

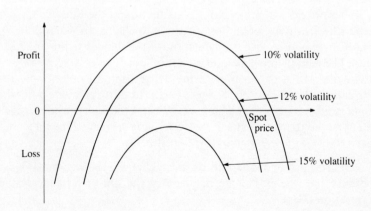

Hedging using options

3.6 'Vega' Hedging

It is possible to protect an options position against adverse movements in the volatility of the underlying currency. One method is by using the vega (zeta) factor. Vega is the profit or loss expressed in cash terms derived from a 0.1% change in volatility.

> **Example 3.3 Using Vega**
> Suppose a call option on sterling struck at 1.60 with a volatility of 15% and a spot rate of 1.60 commands a premium of $125,000 on an option covering £5,000,000. Suppose also that the same option, given an implied volatility of 15.1%, would be priced at $125,970 to cover the same £5,000,000. The position would therefore have a vega of $(125,970 - 125,000) = \$970$.
>
> If the same calculation on a 1.65 call gave a vega of $830, the ratio of vega between the 1.60 and 1.65 calls would be 1:1.16867. To create a vega neutral hedge on a short position of £5,000,000 of 1.60 calls, we would have to buy £5,843,350 of 1.65 calls. If volatility were to rise, then the loss incurred on the short position of 1.60 calls could be offset by the rise in value of the 1.65 calls. If this reasoning is combined with a delta neutral position to neutralise the risk of loss through movements in the underlying currency, then all the risk reward potential of an options position is covered – a rather futile exercise perhaps. However, insulated from price and volatility a trader could profit from his bid–offer spread.
>
> Clearly, managing an options position can be a very complex and hazardous procedure. Consequently, it is essential to monitor the situation continuously. It is possible to give a quantitative valuation to the level of difficulty in managing an options position using the 'gamma'.

3.7 Gamma

The gamma provides a numerical approximation of the rate of change of the delta (the sensitivity of an options value to changes in volatility). The gamma is also used to give an indication of the difficulty in managing a position. The gamma movement of an option portfolio is typically referred to in either positive or negative terms. In general, an options position gamma cannot be too positive. Rather, it is the negative characteristics that are significant. A high negative gamma indicates the high sensitivity of the overall portfolio to movements in the underlying currency. The three main characteristics of the gamma are explained below:

1. The shorter the time to expiration, the higher will be the gamma. This is because the rate of change in value of the option will increase as expiration nears.

32

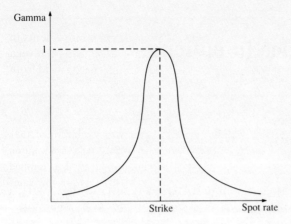

Figure 3.3 The gamma

2. At-the-money, options have the highest gammas in relation to other options in the same expiration period. Figure 3.3 indicates that close to the strike price a small movement in the underlying price produces a sharp increase in the option value (volatility increases as the spot price approaches the strike price). As a result the value of the delta is changing most rapidly at this point, hence the gamma values are greatest.
3. The gamma of a put and call option of the same expiration and strike price will have approximately the same value. Consequently, it would be of equal difficulty to manage, say, a short position in either on a delta basis.

Apart from reducing exposure, traders will endeavour to realise profits by efficient management of their portfolios. The strategies commonly used to exploit potentially profitable situations are discussed in the next chapter.

CHAPTER 4

Strategies in options

4.1 Introduction

In managing their portfolios, options traders will constantly be looking for opportunities to make a profit through arbitrage with other foreign exchange markets. In an efficient market it should be impossible to make a profit from the price differentials that exist between the forward and option markets. This would imply that the difference between the call and put premiums for any option with the same exercise price would be equal to the difference between the forward exchange rate and the exercise price, discounted by the market interest rate. This relationship is called the call–put parity. However, arbitrage opportunities do exist occasionally and can be exploited.

4.2 Synthetics

The two main strategies in this area are known as a 'reversal' and a 'conversion'. They involve the creation of artificial forward contracts either to buy or sell the underlying currency using put and call options.

A reversal is created when a trader simultaneously buys a call and sells a put option for the same expiration date and exercise price. This gives the trader the same pattern of gains and losses as he would have on a forward contract to purchase the same currency on the same expiration date, and at the same exercise (strike) price. By buying a call and selling a put, the trader is effectively purchasing the currency forward. If the cost of buying the currency in this way is cheaper than buying it under a normal forward contract, the trader can make a profit by following the reversal with a forward sale. Figure 4.1 shows the P/L profiles for a forward purchase of, say, £100,000 at 1.60 and a purchase of £100,000 calls at $0.015/£ (both struck at 1.60).

Alternatively, if the cost of buying the currency under a forward contract is cheaper than obtaining it through the use of puts and calls, the trader can make a profit by carrying out the opposite of a reversal – a conversion. Here

34

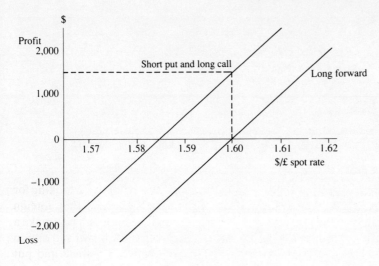

Figure 4.1   Forward purchases of the underlying currency against a short
put and long call position

the option trader could create an artificial contract to sell the currency
forward by buying a put and selling a call (Figure 4.2). Once again the
premium for the call is $0.015/£, and the premium for the put is $0.03/£ so
an immediate debit of $1,500 is established by choosing the synthetic route.
However, after taking into account interest rate differentials, bid–offer
spreads and commission on the forward contract, the option route could
still turn out to be more cost-effective in certain circumstances.

Synthetics are also useful for traders with an unbalanced portfolio of calls
and puts, even if there are no opportunities for arbitrage profits. Traders
can change existing call options into puts, or vice-versa, by using the
forward market. Normally a trader will aim to match calls and puts in an
option portfolio, but synthetics could prove a useful strategy to balance any
mis-matched positions.

4.3   Combinations of Options

Besides the reversal and conversion there are other strategies which involve
combinations of puts and calls. The extent to which they are used is
dependent upon the trader's view of the market.

Suppose the trader believes that sterling is bullish and accordingly is
going to rise appreciably against the dollar. He must then choose which call
option or combination of call options to buy. In choosing, he will need to
resolve the following questions. Should he buy at-the-money, in-the-money

Strategies in options

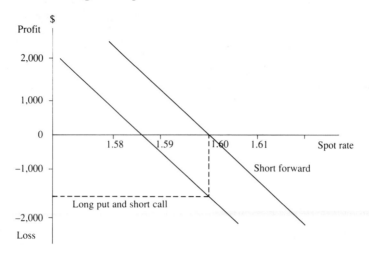

Figure 4.2 Forward sale of the underlying currency against a long put and short call position

or out-of-the-money calls? Should they be short maturity or long maturity options?

Given that the current spot rate is 1.60, an investor who believes that the exchange rate will rise only moderately will be unlikely to buy out-of-the money $1.63 calls. Conversely, an investor who is expecting a major shift in the exchange rate might regard this option as very attractive. It must also be remembered that the time frame of the traders exchange rate forecast is as important as the forecast itself.

4.4 Vertical Spreads

One strategy of use in the case of a bullish rate forecast is simultaneously to buy and sell vertical spreads of options with different strike prices. This is illustrated in Figure 4.3 which assumes a spot sterling rate of $1.60, buy $1.63 call at a premium of 2 cents and write (sell) $1.68 at a premium of 0.4 cents. Neither option could be exercised at spot prices below $1.63 and the trader will make a net loss equal to the balance of the premiums $(0.4 - 2.0 = -1.6$ cents per £1). As the value of sterling increases beyond $1.63 there is a potential gain from buying sterling at the strike price of $1.63 and then selling it at a profit. This potential gain increases until it reaches 5 cents per £1 when the exchange rate is $1.68. The net gain at $1.68 taking into account the net premium is $5 - 1.6 = 3.4$ cents per £1. As the price of sterling increases beyond $1.68 the $1.68 call option will be

36

exercised, obliging the trader to buy at $1.63 while selling at a higher price. Therefore, as the price of sterling increases beyond $1.68 the additional gains from exercising the $1.63 call are cancelled by the losses on the $1.68 call, leaving the net profit at a constant 1.6 cents per £1.

Such a spread may attract a trader who is either risk aversive or believes that sterling is likely to strengthen to around $1.68 and then level out. Effectively, it involves the trader sacrificing any profit that might arise from the spot price of sterling rising above $1.68 but would reduce his premium payments, and therefore risk, by 0.4 cents per £1.

Conversely a hedger who believes that sterling will not strengthen beyond $1.68 but is seeking to insure against a rise in spot above $1.63 might also find this vertical spread attractive. The writing of the $1.68 call enables gains from the $1.63 call to be offset by losses on the $1.68 call but with the advantage that the premium paid is reduced by 0.4 cents per £1.

This strategy also raises the interesting point of how hedging can involve elements of trading: the view taken on the likely movement of the future exchange rates is indicative of hedging, whereas selling the $1.68 call option is effectively trading, based on the assumption that sterling will not strengthen beyond $1.68.

When the trader anticipates a weakening in the price of sterling (a bearish sterling market) a vertical hedged strategy, involving elements of trading, could be utilised using puts. For example, if we assume the same spot rate of

Figure 4.3   Profit and loss on a bull call spread

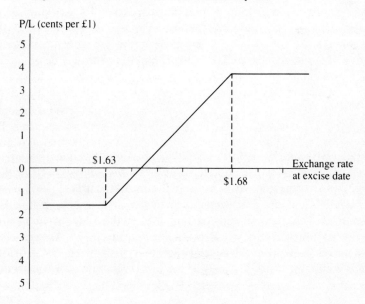

$1.60, the trader could buy a $1.58 put at a premium of 3.5 cents and write a $1.55 put at a premium of 0.5 cents. Such a strategy might be attractive to a trader who believes that the price of sterling will fall towards $1.55 but is unlikely to fall below this. Similarly, a hedger wanting to insure against the possibility of sterling depreciating below $1.58, but holding the view that it will not go below $1.55, could use such a strategy. Effectively, the net premium payable is reduced from 3.5 to 3.0 cents per £1 at a cost of foregoing protection from depreciation below $1.55.

Vertical strategies involving bullish put spreads and bearish call spreads could also be considered. If a speculator anticipated sterling appreciating relative to the US dollar, possible gains could come from buying a put option with a low strike price (and low premium) and writing a put option with a high strike price (and high premium). If sterling did subsequently appreciate, such a strategy would produce a gain equal to the difference between the two premiums, since neither option would be exercised if the price exceeded the higher strike price.

If sterling was expected to depreciate relative to the US dollar a bearish call spread would be considered. This would involve buying a call option with a high strike price (and low premium) and writing a call option with a low strike price (and high premium). If sterling did depreciate in value below the lower strike price neither option would be exercised and the difference between the premiums would constitute the profit.

4.5 Volatility Forecast Trades

The responsiveness of option premiums to volatility introduces a new trading feature based on the ability to trade on expectations about exchange rates. By taking a position on future exchange rates a combination of options can be used to yield profits either above or below a certain price and maintain losses within an acceptable level. Three strategies typically used in this way are straddles, strangles and butterflies.

Straddles

A trader who anticipates low volatility (stable exchange rates) may well sell a straddle, which involves simultaneously writing (selling) both a call and a put option at the same strike price. In Figure 4.4 the strike price is assumed to be $1.60 and the P/L profile is indicated by the broken line. If the exchange rate were to remain constant at $1.60 the trader would maximise his profits, which in our example would be 0.3 cents per £1. As the exchange rate moves away from this level, profitability is reduced, but provided it keeps within the range $1.55–$1.65 the loss on the currency transaction is

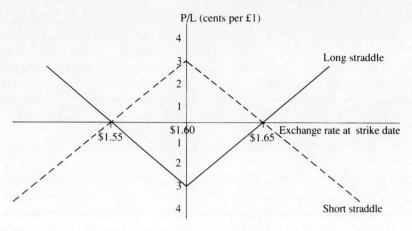

P/L (cents per £1)

Figure 4.4 Profit and loss on long and short straddles

less than the sum of the premiums and the writer of the straddle makes a profit.

Conversely, expectations of high volatility may well lead a trader to buy a straddle. If the expectations are justified and sterling deviates by more than 0.3 cents from the strike price of $1.60 the trader will make a net gain. However, if the price of sterling deviates by less than 0.3 cents or at the worst remains at $1.60, a total of 0.3 cents per £1 would have been paid in premiums with no offsetting gains from currency transactions.

Strangles

A strangle involves buying or writing simultaneous put and call options on the same currency and expiry date but at different strike prices. In Figure 4.5 a long strangle is represented by the broken line. A trader anticipating considerable volatility could simultaneously buy a call option with a strike price of $1.65 and a put option with a strike price of $1.55. The sum of the two premiums is 2 cents per £1. If the price of sterling remains within the range $1.55–$1.65 the trader makes a net loss equal to the sum of the premiums. Exchange rate movements outside this range, however, provide the trader with a potential gain from the currency transactions that offset the cost of the premiums. For example, a spot price of $1.52 would produce a profit of 3 cents per £1 from the $1.55 put option, which would more than offset the cost of 2 cents per £1.

A trader anticipating low volatility might sell a short strangle as indicated by the unbroken line in Figure 4.5. This strategy is the opposite of

39

Strategies in options

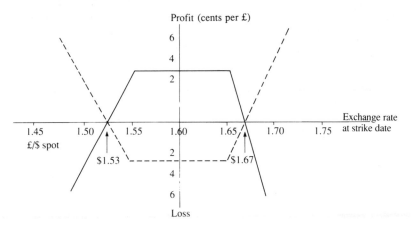

Figure 4.5   Profit and loss on long and short strangles

the above and involves simultaneously selling a call and a put option at different strike prices. We have again assumed strike prices of $1.55 and $1.65, respectively, and a 2 cents per £1 net premium. Variations of sterling spot rate within this range will produce potential gains to the trader, whereas variations outside the range will result in a loss.

Butterfly Spread

To create a short butterfly spread the trader would write an in-the-money call, buy two at-the-money calls and write an out-of-the-money call. Conversely, to create a long butterfly spread the trader would buy an in-the-money call, sell two at-the-money calls and buy an out-of-the-money call, all with the same expiration date.

Figure 4.6 illustrates a P/L profile for a long butterfly spread based upon the following assumptions:

Sterling spot rate = $1.60.

Buy 1, $1.55 call – premium of 5.0 cents
Sell 2, $1.60 calls – premium of 2.7 cents
Buy 1, $1.65 call – premium of 1.2 cents

At spot prices below $1.55, none of the options would be exercised and the trader would make a loss of 1 cent per £1, which is equivalent to the excess of premiums paid over those received. As the spot price moves from $1.55 towards $1.60 there is a cent-for-cent gain from the currency

40

transaction, equal to a net profit of 4 cents per £1 at $1.60. Further increases in the price of sterling would result in the cent-for-cent losses on the two written options outweighing the gains from the $1.55 long call. When spot eventually reaches $1.65 the 10 cent gain from the $1.55 long call is exactly offset by the two 5 cent losses arising from the $1.60 short calls. At a spot rate of $1.65, therefore, the net position is back to a loss of 1 cent per £1. As the price of sterling increases beyond $1.65, the $1.65 long call would be exercised resulting in a cent-for-cent gain from two long calls and a corresponding loss from two short calls. The result would be that for prices in excess of £1.65 the trader would make a net loss of 1 cent per £1.

Once again this butterfly strategy is useful if the trader expects the currency to remain within a certain range, in our example $1.56–$1.64.

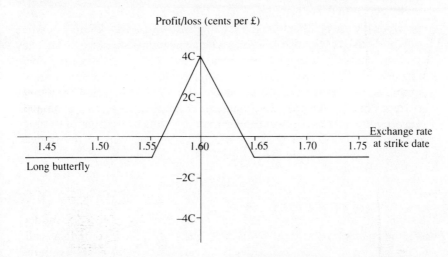

Figure 4.6   Profit and loss on long butterfly spread

The attraction of these alternative strategies is that they enable the trader to control the timing of the exercise of the options they have written. A choice between the alternatives themselves is very much determined by the trader's expectations about volatility and his attitude towards risk. Table 4.1 identifies the main determinants in choosing a strategy. At one extreme a straddle is attractive to a trader with a confident view on the likely future movements of exchange rates. The profit potential is high but so, too, is the risk of loss if exchange rates differ from expectations. At the other extreme, a butterfly spread is attractive to a trader with a much less confident view on likely future exchange rates. This strategy is the least risky as it limits potential losses and gains within a lower and an upper limit.

41

Strategies in options

Table 4.1. Determinants of strategy

Strategy type	Volatility	Risk/return
Straddle	Confident	High risk/high profit
Strangle	Less confident	Less risk/less profit
Butterfly	Least confident	Least risk/least profit

4.6   Conclusions

Currency options provide cover over a wide range of strike prices and expiration dates. They can be obtained on both listed and OTC markets and their use in either hedging or speculative strategies does not necessarily preclude the use of other foreign exchange instruments. By limiting possible downside risk to a known amount and levying premium up-front, currency options enable a buyer to incorporate costs and risks into his pricing formula, while still retaining the possibility of upside gain from favourable exchange rate movements. Options are also ideal for hedging contingent currency flows when both the timing and completion of the transaction are uncertain.

CHAPTER 5

Traded currency options

5.1 Introduction

In contrast to over-the-counter (OTC) options, traded options are standardised. Although the standardisation ensures adequate liquidity in the market, it does lead corporate users to prefer the relatively more expensive OTC options, provided mainly by the banks. This is due largely to the fact that they can be tailor-made to suit the individual needs of the corporate customers. Conversely, banks tend to prefer traded options which can be used to offset the OTC options, provided to customers.

5.2 Standardisation

Currency options are traded on a number of exchanges throughout the world, against several major currencies. In the United States they are actively traded on the Chicago Board Options Exchange (cash), Philadelphia Stock Exchange (cash) and Chicago Mercantile Exchange (futures). Elsewhere they are traded on the European Options Exchange in Amsterdam (cash), the Montreal Exchange (cash), the Vancouver Exchange (cash) and the Sydney Futures Exchange (cash). In England they are traded on LIFFE (futures) and the London Stock Exchange (cash), either for sterling against US dollars, US dollars against Deutschmarks or Deutschmarks against US dollars.

On LIFFE, the sterling option (i.e. sterling against US dollars) is traded in blocks of £25,000, the exercise prices are at intervals of 5 cents (i.e. $1.60, $1.65, $1.70, $1.75 per £1) and there are just five expiry dates available at any one time, i.e. a date in the three nearest months followed by the earliest month in the March, June, September, December cycle. Expiry dates occur two business days before the third Wednesday of the expiry month and premiums are quoted in US cents per £1 with a tick size of 0.01 cents per £1 (i.e. $2.50).

5.3 Market Practices

With traded options, in particular, a hedger is likely to sell his options rather than to exercise them. For instance, if spot was $1.75, an exporter anticipating dollars in, say, seven weeks' time could buy a sterling call option with an exercise price of $1.75 and a premium of 2 cents per £1. If when the exporter received his dollars the pound had strengthened to $1.80, he could either exercise the options and pay $1.75 per £1, plus the premium, making a total of $1.77 per £1 for sterling, or sell the options. The strengthening of the pound relative to the dollar would increase the market value of $1.75 call options and premiums could, therefore, rise to 6 cents per £1. The hedger could, therefore, sell his options at a profit of 4 cents per £1 and then buy sterling at the new spot price of $1.80. The effective price of sterling would then be $1.80 − $0.040 = $1.76 per £1.

Clearly, this ability to sell options and profit in this way ensures a buoyant trading market based essentially upon views as to future changes in market expectations of volatility and views on the speed of exchange rate movements. Increased exchange rate volatility tends to increase the probability of options being exercised profitably and, therefore, causes option writers to require higher premiums. Similarly, option buyers attracted by the prospect of realising profits are usually quite prepared to pay higher premiums.

5.4 Margins on Traded Currency Options

Like currency futures, traded currency options have margins based upon exactly the same principles, incorporating an initial and variation margin. The initial margin for a traded currency option position, however, is determined by estimating its risk from a risk factor (delta) which is calculated daily by the Exchange for all traded options. This is referred to as the 'delta bound' margining systems. The risk factor is then multiplied by the relevant currency futures margin to obtain the initial margin for the currency options position.

In contrast to the initial margin on a currency future, which remains constant until delivery, the initial margin on a currency option will vary in accordance with the risk factor. For a short option positions an additional prudential risk margin is usually required. However, there is full and automatic offset of initial margins between options and futures – options combinations.

Example 5.1 indicates the cashflow involved with initial and variation margins for the purchase of two (£25,000) sterling call options. The example assumes an initial margin of $US500, which equates with the equivalent sterling currency futures margin shown in Example 7.1 (Chapter 7).

Example 5.1 Option initial margin

Buy 1 June 1.60 call, risk factor = 0.70

Buy 1 June 1.65 call, risk factor = 0.50

Number of futures equivalent contracts = 0.7 + 0.5 = 1.20

Required initial margin = $500 × 1.2 = $600

Option variation margin

Day 1

June $1.65 call premium = 3.20 cents, risk factor = 0.45

Buyer's initial margin $500 × 0.5   = $250

Seller's initial margin $500 × 0.5   = $250

Plus illustrative prudential add-on = $100

                              $350

Day 2

June $1.65 call premium = 2.75 cents, risk factor = 0.45

Buyer's variation margin (2.75–3.20) − 0.45 cents

45 basis points at $2.50 per basis point = $112.50

Reduction in buyer's initial margin requirement: $250 − ($500 × 0.45) = $25

Buyer's net cash flow = − $62.50 (− $112.50 + $25)

Seller's net cash flow = + $112.50 + $25 = $137.50

The risk factor approach can be easily extended to portfolios of futures and options contracts. The risk factor for a portfolio of futures and options positions is simply the absolute value of the sum of the risk factors of the individual positions.

5.5 Delta Hedge (Ratio Hedge)

A delta hedge with options is designed to maintain a combined cash and options position with a zero delta through time on a continuous basis (delta neutral strategy). Such a hedge may need frequent rebalancing and will be more risky than a fixed hedge because the number of options required will be larger. The most typical case of ratio hedging is the hedging of an OTC currency option written by a bank or financial institution.

Example 5.2 Ratio hedging using currency options

Suppose a bank sells a dollar–Deutschmark six month call option on $5,000,000 with an exercise price of DM 1.91 to a customer for a premium of DM 312,500. Using the implied volatilities from current LIFFE premiums, the fair price of the option equals DM 273,000 and the option delta is 0.4372. The bank has thereby generated a potential profit of

Traded currency options

DM 39,500 (DM 312,500 − DM 273,000) and wishes to protect this profit.

The bank thus hedges the written option position by purchasing LIFFE December DM 1.90 dollar–Deutschmark call options.

Option premium = 5.92 pfennigs (pf)
Implied delta = 0.4604

$$\text{Number of options contracts:} \quad \frac{\$5,000,000}{\$50,000} \times \frac{0.4372}{0.4604} = 95 \text{ contracts}$$

Buy 95 DM 1.90 calls at 5.92 pf.
Cost = 0.0592 × $50,000 × 95 = DM 281,200

Suppose in one weeks' time the situation is as follows:

Dollar–Deutschmark spot = 1.9243
Dollar–Deutschmark forward = 1.9065
Fair price of OTC DM 1.90 call = DM 317,850
Implied delta = 0.4953

OTC fair price difference = DM 44,850 (317,850 − 273,000) (Loss to bank)

LIFFE DM 1.90 December call premium = 6.87 pf
Implied delta = 0.5168

LIFFE options profit = 95 × 50,000 × (DM 0.0687 − DM 0.0592)
= DM 45,125

Net hedge gain = DM 45,125 − DM 44,850 = DM 275
Bank's expected profit is now DM 39,500 + DM 275 = DM 39,775

This ratio hedge was designed to be delta neutral but did not work perfectly because the hedge ratio changed over time. Nevertheless, it is certainly more effective and manageable than a hedge using LIFFE futures contracts. It is also worth noting that this type of ratio hedge needs to be continually rebalanced to keep the hedge as near riskless as possible. The hedge performance can be affected by changes in implied volatility, a feature that applies to all options hedges.

5.6 Providing Fixed Rate Funds in Other Currencies

For banks the availability of both interest rate futures contracts and foreign exchange rate futures contracts provides a means to lend funds in currencies other than dollars or sterling at fixed rates in the future.

Example 5.3 Fixed Rate Funds
Suppose on 10 December a customer asks the bank to quote a fixed rate for Deutschmark funds for the period 16 March–16 September. The

46

Fixed rate funds in other currencies

Table 5.1. Sample futures prices

	March	June	September
$/DM	0.5348	0.5385	0.5420
Eurodollar time deposit	92.77	92.32	91.96

current futures prices on LIFFE are as shown in Table 5.1. First the bank would calculate the swap price, i.e. the cost of simultaneously selling dollars at one date and buying them back at a subsequent date, for the two periods March–June and June–September.

$$\text{Swap price} = \frac{\text{\$/DM rate (date 1)} - \text{\$/DM rate (date 2)}}{\text{\$/DM rate (date 1)} \times (\text{No. of days}/360)} \times 100$$

$$\text{Swap price (\$/DM) 16 March–16 June} = \frac{0.5348 - 0.5385}{0.5348 \times (92/360)} \times 100$$

$$= -2.707\% \text{ per annum}$$

$$\text{Swap price (\$/DM) 16 June–16 September} = \frac{0.5385 - 0.5420}{0.5385 \times (92/360)} \times 100$$

$$= -2.543\% \text{ per annum}$$

Given these swap prices, the bank would then determine the costs of DM funds for the March–June period and the June–September period. The transactions would be carried out in the following manner:

10 December
March–June: buy March DM at 0.5348
             Sell June DM at 0.5385

Swap price = −2.707%pa. (i.e. the effective annualised gain on obtaining DMs for the three month period March–June)
Sell March Eurodollar at 92.77 – locks in an annualised interest rate of 7.23% for lending dollars for the three months, March–June
Net cost of DM borrowing = 7.23% − 2.707% = 4.523%

June–September
Buy June DM at 0.5385
Sell September DM at 0.5420
Swap price = −2.543%

Sell June Eurodollar at 92.32 – locks in an annualised interest rate of 7.68% for lending dollars for the three months June–September
Net cost of DM borrowing = 7.68 − 2.543 = 5.137%

Assuming that interest on the DM borrowing is paid quarterly and that

47

Traded currency options

Table 5.2. Sample swap and cash rates

	Cash DM-3 month Euro rate	$/DM swap March–June	$/DM swap June–September	March Eurodollar	June Eurodollar
16 March	5.29%	−2.064%		92.64	
16 June	5.51%		−1.95%		92.54

Actual borrowing costs

16 March   Buy March Eurodollar at 92.64. Gain=0.13%

Unwind March/June DM spread. Bought at swap price = (2.707%)
Sold at swap price = (2.064%)
Gain = 0.643%
Combined gain = 0.13 + 0.643 = 0.77%
Cash Euro DM rate = 5.29%
Net borrowing of DM funds = (5.29 − 0.77) = 4.52%

16 June   Buy Eurodollar at 92.54. Loss = 0.22%

Unwind June/September DM spread. Bought at swap price = (2.543%)
Sold at swap price = (1.95%)
Gain = 0.59%
Combined Gain = 0.59 − 0.22 = 0.37%
Cash Euro DM rate = 5.51%
Net borrowing cost of DM funds = 5.51 − 0.37 = 5.14%

the bank wants a 75 basis point spread, the bank would be in a position to quote a fixed annual rate for 16 March in December of (4.523 + 5.137)/2 + 0.75 = 5.58%.

How this hedge may resolve itself in practice is shown in Table 5.2. Assume that the set of prices given in Table 5.2 apply on 16 March and 16 June respectively. The net effective cost of borrowing DM funds to provide the fixed rate funds to the customer was virtually identical to the cost originally estimated. This is because basis risk is virtually eliminated by the closeness of the lending date to the delivery dates of the LIFFE Eurodollar contract. Although the assumptions made in this example may not always hold and adverse variation margin payments may be necessary, it is apparent that the financial futures markets may provide commercial banks with opportunities for fixed rate lending in currencies other than those in which interest rate futures contracts are denominated.

CHAPTER 6

The break forward contract

6.1 Introduction

At the end of 1986 a new foreign exchange hedging instrument appeared in the market: the break forward contract, developed in response to the need of exporters, importers, borrowers and investors, to hedge against persistent volatility in exchange and interest rates. The break forward is a forward foreign exchange contract which can be unwound at a predetermined rate. It combines the most attractive features of traditional forward contracts and currency options. Like forward contracts, break forwards allow the customer to hedge against adverse exchange rate movements by locking into a fixed rate.

6.2 Features of Break Forward Contracts

1. *Certainty*

Like forward contracts, break forwards allow the customer to hedge against adverse exchange rate movements by locking in a fixed rate.

2. *No Up-Front Payment*

Unlike options which require up-front payment of a premium, all costs are incorporated into the fixed rate.

3. *Flexibility*

Unlike traditional forward contracts, the customer can benefit from favourable exchange rate movements by breaking the forward deal, and then dealing at spot. They also allow the customer to choose the fixed rate by agreeing to a loading on the normal outright forward rate. The bank can then calculate the rate at which the forward deal can be unwound, typically referred to as the break rate. Alternatively, the customer can nominate the break rate and the bank will then calculate the fixed rate.

The break forward contract

Break forwards also allow the customer continuously to monitor his hedge and unwind it if the current forward rate becomes advantageous. If the funds are required early, or received early, then they can be bought or sold spot and the forward deal can be unwound at the break rate.

6.3 Applications

Take the case of export cover: a UK corporate treasurer due to receive dollars in the future would normally sell forward to lock in his profit, but the break forward also enables him to take advantage of favourable exchange rate movements. Similarly, in the case of a tender for an export contract, a break forward contract can avoid the open ended commitment and unlimited potential loss of a traditional forward contract in the event of failing to secure the contract.

In the case of importers, the fixed rate protects against a sterling depreciation. The break facility then allows buyers of foreign currency, such as tour operators for instance, to benefit from favourable movements in the market.

Example 6.1 How to calculate the break rate

Suppose a UK importer anticipates making payment of $1 million in three months' time and normally covers all foreign exchange exposures by using the traditional forward market. The importers concern would be two-fold: firstly, if he locks into a forward rate he would be unable to benefit from a favourable market; and, secondly, if he does not need to make the full anticipated payment of $1,000,000 he would be exposed to a foreign exchange loss.

If the current spot rate was 1.5300 and the forward premium points 100, the outright forward price would be 1.5200 giving a cost of £657,894 in three months' time. Conversely, if the customer entered into a break forward contract for three months to buy dollars and sell sterling, he may, for instance, request a fixed rate to be set at a 2% loading on the forward rate. The pricing would then be arrived at as follows:

Spot	1.5300
3 month forward points	− 100
Outright forward	1.5200
Break loading	− 0.0304(− 0.02 × 1.5200)
Fixed rate	1.4896

The bank calculates the break rate at 1.5500.

Table 6.1. Effect of moving market on break forward contract

Spot rate, 3 months time	Break forward (£)	Traditional forward (£)	Net saving (£)
1.50	671,321	657,894	(13,427)
1.55	671,321	657,894	(13,247)
1.5816 (break even)	657,894	657,894	0
1.60	650,342	657,894	7,552
1.65	630,634	675,894	27,260
1.70	612,086	657,894	45,808
1.75	594,598	657,894	63,296

Note: based on the same assumptions as in Example 6.1.

If the dollar was stronger than the break rate of 1.55, i.e. 1.50, the customer would merely transact at the agreed fixed rate of $1.4896. If the dollar was equal to or weaker than the break rate of $1.55, i.e. 1.60 on maturity, the break facility would be activated: the customer would still buy $1,000,000 at the fixed rate but would now sell back the £1 million at the break rate and then buy the $1,000,000 at spot.

The break facility can be activated at any time the dollar weakens below the break rate, enabling the customer to buy at the prevailing forward rate. He can, therefore, insure against a sizeable adverse exchange rate movement with no up-front cost and retain the opportunity for unlimited profit if the exchange rate moves in his favour.

6.4 Comparison with Forward Contacts

A traditional forward exchange contract at $1.52 would cost the customer £657,894 in three months, irrespective of exchange rate movements. In comparison, a break forward contract with the fixed rate at $1.4896 could produce considerable savings (see Table 6.1). An added advantage, of course, is that the break forward can be activated at any time.

6.5 Conclusion

The innovative break forward contracts confer the ability to profit if the market moves favourably without the cost of an option premium. Loss is also limited to the difference between the fixed rate and the forward rate.

CHAPTER 7

Currency futures

7.1 Introduction

Foreign currency futures were the first type of financial futures contract. They were introduced on the International Commercial Exchange (ICE) in 1970, but were never actively traded with the result that the ICE rapidly went out of business. In 1972, the Chicago Mercantile Exchange, followed by the New York Mercantile Exchange in 1974, were the first exchanges successfully to introduce foreign currency contracts. Interest rate futures contracts were subsequently introduced in 1975 on the Chicago Board of Trade and the Chicago Mercantile Exchange, following their designation by the Commodity Futures Trading Commission.

Currently, financial futures are actively traded on the Sydney Futures Exchange in Australia, the Toronto and Montreal Exchanges in Canada, the London International Financial Futures Exchange in the United Kingdom and the Chicago Board of Trade, the Chicago Mercantile Exchange (International Monetary Market) and the Mid-American Commodity Exchange in the United States.

Although contract specifications obviously vary according to each exchange, the fundamentals of financial futures and the basic principles underlying the dynamics of trading and hedging are essentially the same, irrespective of location. Nevertheless, to facilitate ease of presentation and continuity we have elaborated the practices prevalent in the London International Financial Futures Exchange (LIFFE) and based our examples on the financial futures contracts traded on that exchange.

LIFFE provides facilities for dealing in futures contracts including short term interest rates, government bonds, stock indices and foreign currencies and also offers traded options on financial instruments and currencies. It has a membership which is widely representative of the financial service industry and includes: banks, stockbrokers, stockjobbers, commodity brokers, discount houses, Eurobond houses, money brokers and experienced individual traders (known as 'locals') who trade on their own account. Approximately half of the members are individuals or companies based outside the United Kingdom.

7.2 What are financial futures?

A financial futures contract is an agreement to buy or sell, on an organised exchange, a standard quantity of a specific financial instrument, or a foreign currency, at a future rate and at a price agreed between two parties. Contracts are traded between buyers and sellers on the exchange floor and each has an obligation, not to one another but to a clearing house. This ensures that the futures market is largely free from credit risk.

A currency futures contract fixes the effective exchange rate for the exchange of a specific amount of one currency for another at a specific date in the future. On that date, unless the contract has been closed out, both the buyer and seller of the contract have an obligation to take and make delivery of the underlying currency. The position is exactly analogous to a forward exchange rate transaction.

7.3 Standardisation

Currency futures traded on LIFFE include sterling, Deutschmarks, yen, Swiss francs, each being traded against the US dollar. Each type of contract is specified by the Exchange, with the standard contract size for sterling currency contracts, for instance, being £25,000 (DM 125,000, SF 125,000, Y 12,500,000). For all currencies, maturity dates coincide with the March, June, September and December cycles and delivery takes place on the third Wednesday of the delivery month.

The tick size for a currency futures contract is 0.01 cents per £1. This is the smallest change in the price of a futures contract permitted by LIFFE. Each tick has a specific money value which is $2.50 for sterling $(0.0001 \times 25,000 = 2.50)$ and $12.50 for other currencies. The initial margin varies between currencies but they are all deemed to be deliverable in the principal financial centres of the country of issue. This standardisation of contracts greatly enhances the liquidity of the market and thereby ensures easy trading conditions.

7.4 Clearing

LIFFE's clearing house – the International Commodities Clearing House (ICCH), not only clears but guarantees the exchange transactions. Consequently, the clearing function is a particularly important facet of the market. Essentially, it has three main purposes:

1. Traders on the exchange obviously trade with each other but ICCH becomes a counterparty to every futures position by substituting itself for both parties. This largely eliminates credit risk for traders and allows the 'open outcry' system to operate successfully.

2. Clearing also makes trading easier and facilitates the 'closing out' of transactions by opposite transactions. For example, if you have sold an option, then the obligation can be voided by simply buying an option with an identical exercise price and expiration date. It then becomes necessary to run two equal and opposite positions until expiry or exercise.
3. The clearing house safeguards its exposure by requiring members to deposit cash or collateral (margin – see Section 7.11) to cover the risk of movement in exchange rates. Alternatively, collateral in the form of government stock or bank guarantees may be deposited with ICCH. Interest arising from these deposits is still paid to the contract holder.

7.5   How the Futures Market Works

In the LIFFE market contracts have just four maturity dates. For example, in, say, February, one would be trading sterling currency contracts for delivery in either March, September, December or March. The contract month nearest the current date is usually referred to as the 'nearby month'. Once that contract month has begun it is referred to as the 'spot month'. Experience to date in London has revealed that most business is transacted in the 'nearby' contract.

The dealing method is by 'open outcry' whereby traders meet in recessed octagonal pits and shout out their bids and offers in order to match buyers and sellers. Once transactions have been made they are recorded in writing by both parties, reported to the market officials, and quickly fed into the markets computer. This computer is linked with the futures market price display system and to Reuters and Telerate, etc. The price at which a trade is done will thus be known throughout the world in a matter of seconds after it is transacted.

7.6   Trading

A trader attempts to profit from increases or decreases in the underlying contract, having first taken a view as to likely future changes. The futures market facilitates this process by enabling a trader either to buy or sell a futures contract and thereby adopt the stance he wishes to take without actually having to buy or sell the underlying currency or financial future.

Some traders, referred to as 'tick traders', make very rapid transactions throughout the day in an attempt to make small profits (typically one or two ticks) on each deal. By the end of the trading day no position is held but by the sheer volume of individual deals a healthy profit is realised. Similarly, a 'day trader' aims to finish the day without a position, but rather than going for high volume activity he takes an overall view of the market during the course of the day and trades accordingly. A longer term perspective of the market is taken by a 'position trader', who trades with the objective of establishing a market position that will eventually realise a profit.

7.7 Hedging

Hedging is the process of protecting a position against risk from adverse exchange rate or interest rate movements. By buying a sterling futures contract, for instance, a UK exporter could protect himself from any future depreciation of the US dollar. By definition, the process of buying a futures contract involves another party selling exactly the same rights and obligations. In this sense hedging involves a transfer of risk. The seller of a sterling futures contract may be either a hedger wishing to avoid the opposite risk, i.e. an appreciation in the value of sterling relative to the US dollar, or a speculator willing to incur the risk in the expectation of making a profit.

7.8 Speculating

In all probability the value of hedging against one particular direction of exchange rate movement will not be exactly matched by the value of hedging against the opposite direction. The UK exporter in our example will not necessarily find sufficient hedgers wishing to avoid an appreciation of the US dollar. Fortunately, liquidity in futures is provided by the activity of speculators who deal in the market with a view to making profits. If the futures price is above the speculators' own expectations they will sell in the anticipation of subsequently buying back at a lower price. Conversely, if the futures price is below speculators' expectations they will buy futures in anticipation of subsequently selling at a higher price.

Hedgers who wish to buy more sterling futures than are currently available marginally increase the price and induce the speculator to sell and realise a profit. An excess of hedgers wishing to sell sterling futures will marginally depress the price, causing speculators to buy. In this way, speculators provide liquidity within the futures market.

7.9 Closing Out

Hedgers do not need to hold futures contracts until maturity and can either buy or sell at any time. In practice they are frequently 'closed out' (cancelled), especially as standardised maturity dates invariably do not coincide with the underlying import or export contract. The UK exporter in our preceding example, anticipating dollar receipts in, say, four months' time, may hedge by buying a six month (say December) sterling future. If when the dollars are received the rise in the value of sterling is matched by a rise in the price of December sterling futures, then the hedge will have been successful and he would sell the December future at a profit. This profit from the purchase and subsequent sale of futures will be just enough to offset the loss on the US dollar receivables resulting from the exchange rate movement.

7.10   Basis

The price difference between the futures and the cash contract being hedged is known as the basis. Where the spot and the future price moves exactly in line (as in the above example), basis is zero. Any change in basis would render the hedge incomplete and result in the hedger making either a loss or a profit depending upon exchange rate movements.

7.11   Margins

In contrast to the cash market, futures are always dealt on margin, which means that only a small proportion of the quoted futures price needs to be paid by the trader. There are two forms of margin – the initial (or original) margin and the variation margin – both of which are settled via the ICCH.

The initial margin which varies in size according to the individual contract is the initial amount required when an investor buys or sells a futures contract. The purpose is to provide a cash buffer against potential losses.

To explain the variation margin it is first necessary to understand the mechanism by which currency futures are settled. With securities markets, profits and losses are only taken when positions are finally 'closed-out'. In the currency futures markets, however, all positions are valued daily on the basis of the exchanges closing official settlement price – a process known as 'marking-to-market'. Profits and losses resulting from the day's change in prices are consequently credited or debited to the investor's account. Any adverse trading position will be rectified by the investor by the payment of additional variation margin. This feature, together with the cushion provided by the initial margin, is effective in preventing and curtailing over-stretched loss positions.

The cash flows involved with initial and variation margins are shown in Example 7.1, which involves a single transaction to purchase a sterling currency contract.

Pricing a currency futures contract

Example 7.1 Margining on futures

Date 24 August 1988
Action: buy One December 1988 Sterling Currency Future at $US1.6500 valuation of this contract = $US41,250 (£25,000 × 1.65). Initial margin paid to clearing house = $US500.

Date 24 August 1988
Closing settlement price = 1.6450 (down 0.0050 on the day). Valuation of this contract = $US41,125. Thus variation margin required by clearing house = $US125. This will return the initial margin back to $US500.

Date 25 August 1988
Closing settlement price = $US1.6320. Valuation of contract = $US40,800. Therefore a variation margin of $US325 will be required by the clearing house.

   If the contractor is not in a position to pay the variation margin then the ICCH has the right to close out his position.

7.12   Pricing a Currency Futures Contract

The fair pricing of a currency futures contract is easily determined. Consider the concept of basis (defined as the difference between the price of the currency in the spot market and the currency futures price). Basis in the currency futures market will simply represent the difference between the Euro interest rates for the two currencies, reflected in a forward discount or premium.

$$\text{Futures currency} = \text{spot rate} \times \left[\frac{1 + \text{Eurodollar interest rate}}{1 + \text{Eurocurrency interest rate}} \right]$$

Example 7.2 Pricing Sterling Currency Futures Contract

Sterling spot rate	=	$1.60
Eurosterling interest rate	=	10%
Eurodollar interest rate	=	$7\frac{1}{2}\%$

$$90 \text{ day forward rate} = \$1.60 \times \left\{ \frac{1 + [0.075 \times (90/365)]}{1 + [0.10 \times (90/365)]} \right\}$$

$$= \$1.59$$

Currency futures

7.13 Hedging with Currency Futures

1. *Cash Market*

Suppose a British exporter signed a contract worth $1,000,000, on 6 May, when the spot exchange rate was £1 = $1.55. At such an exchange rate, the sterling equivalent value of the contract would be £645,161. However, as payment will not take place until 1 August, there is the possibility that the dollar may weaken relative to sterling. If we assume that it did weaken to, say, £1 = $1.65, then the contract would realise a sterling equivalent of £606,061, a loss equivalent to £39,100 ($64,515).

2. *Futures Market*

The exporter in anticipation of a weakening dollar, or as an insurance against such adverse trends, could have hedged his position by buying sterling futures. He would have needed to buy 26 September sterling futures contracts, at £25,000 per contract, at an exchange rate of £1 = $1.55. The total sterling value of the contracts would be £650,000, committing the exporter to a payment of $1,007,500. In the event of the dollar weakening to £1 = $1.65, the exporter would sell the 26 September contracts at $1.65. This would realise $1,072,500 (£650,000 × $1.65) upon maturity of the contracts, giving a gain of $65,000 ($1,072,500 − $1,007,500).

This gain from the futures market offsets the loss from the cash market. The match is clearly not perfect because the £645,161 is combined with £650,000 worth of future contracts. If the cash position was to be adversely affected by a strengthening of the dollar (i.e. the opposite to the above) then the hedge strategy would involve purchasing future currency contracts and realising the profits once the exchange rate has strengthened.

The above example assumes that basis does not change, i.e. the exchange rate in the futures market moves exactly in line with spot. If the two rates change by different amounts, there will be a change in basis making the hedge less perfect.

7.14 Conclusions

In contrast to the currency futures hedge, the options hedge is similar to the purchase of an exchange rate insurance policy rather than an attempt to lock in a specific exchange rate. An example of a fixed hedge was given in Example 3.1, where the full amount of the underlying exposure was hedged with options on a one-to-one basis and closed out when the exposure was removed.

The next chapter examines further the principles of hedging in financial futures and also introduces short-term interest rate futures.

CHAPTER 8

Principles of hedging in financial futures

8.1 Introduction

It has always been possible to secure some protection against future interest rate movements. For example, a company which borrows at fixed rates for six months and deposits the proceeds for the first two months is effectively borrowing 'forward' in two months' time for a period of four months. However, such a strategy has a number of disadvantages compared with a financial futures contract. The build up of liabilities and assets extends the balance sheet and may adversely affect balance sheet measures of company performance. In contrast transactions in interest rate futures are 'off balance sheet'. Hedgers typically close out their positions before taking delivery of the financial instrument and the margin deposit is the only call on their liquidity. Before we look at the individual uses of financial futures contracts we should first examine the basic principles underlying the formation of a hedge.

8.2 Elements in Making the Hedge Decision

1. *Determination of the risk exposure*

The first step in deciding whether to hedge interest or exchange rate risk is to ascertain the level of existing risk. However, this is not simply a matter of considering an individual asset or liability category. A company's balance sheet and operating finances for instance will contain all sorts of natural hedges. These will have to be carefully identified before adopting a hedging strategy in financial futures. Otherwise, a hedging decision, could actually create an open risky position. This is illustrated in Example 8.1 which looks at a simple bank balance sheet.

Example 8.1 Determining balance sheet risk
A bank balance sheet

Liabilities	£(M)	Assets	£(M)
Equity	800	Plant and equipment	300

Principles of hedging in financial futures

Certificates of deposit	1,500	Loans	3,000
Deposit accounts	1,200	Treasury bills	1,000
Current accounts	800		
	4,300		4,300

Assumptions: the certificates of deposit (CDs) and £500,000,000 of the deposit accounts are interest sensitive; the remaining deposit and current accounts are interest insensitive.

2. Interest Rate Risk

From the balance sheet management can construct a net exposed balances table (Table 8.1), which clearly identifies the interest rate risk exposure after the natural hedges have been taken into consideration. The interest rate on £2,000,000,000 of the liabilities will change in the current quarter, but only £500,000,000 of the assets will be re-rated. Effectively, £1,500,000,000 of the liabilities are uncovered for one quarter. During the second quarter, a further £1,000,000,000 of assets will be re-rated leaving £500,000,000 of the liabilities uncovered until the third quarter. Clearly, there is a net exposed liability of £1,500,000,000 to re-finance: £1,000,000,000 will be rolled over once before assets mature and a further £500,000,000 will be rolled over twice.

A possible hedge using financial futures is now evident. The bank could sell £1,500,000,000 of short-term interest rate futures with a delivery date near the end of the next quarter and sell a further £500,000,000 of interest rate futures with a delivery date further out. The balance of net exposed positions after hedging would then appear as shown in Table 8.2. The hedge is now complete: £2,000,000,000 of non-interest sensitive liabilities are matched by £2,000,000,000 of assets. All other interest rate exposure has been hedged, although this does involve the bank in the elements of basis risk.

3. Additional cash flows

A company must also consider additional future cash flows. If it expects funds which will lead to a significant build up of cash in the balance sheet over, say, the next two to three quarters, this will need to be taken into account before implementing a hedging strategy. The net exposed balances table is a dynamic forward looking instrument.

4. Impact of adverse rate changes

Once the composite net exposed balances table has been constructed, the next step is to determine the impact of adverse rate changes. The company

What hedgings are available, and their cost?

Table 8.1. Net exposed balances of a bank by maturity

Maturity (days)	Assets £(M)	Liabilities £(M)	Net exposed balance £(M)	Category
0–90	500	2,000	1,500	Liability
91–180	1,000	0	1,000	Asset
181–270	1,000	0	1,000	Asset
271–365	1,500	0	1,500	Asset
Non-maturity or non-interest sensitive	300	2,300	2,000	Liability

Table 8.2. Net exposed balances after hedging

Maturity (days)	Net exposed balance	Asset or liability
0–90	0	
91–180	0	
181–270	500	Asset
271–365	1,500	Asset
Non-interest sensitive	2,000	Liability

will therefore need to construct a probability distribution of expected future interest rates. This will provide a mean expected interest rate for various periods into the future, and a measure of the probability of interest rates moving adversely.

If we suppose that during the first quarter of the financial year the rate of interest is 9%, a distribution of expected future interest rates could be constructed for the remaining three quarters as shown in Table 8.3. If there is an adverse impact upon the company's financial position from a fall in interest rates, Table 8.3 indicates that a serious interest rate risk exists. This information can be combined with the net exposed balances table to obtain cash values for the risk (Table 8.4). It is these amounts which need to be compared with the cost of hedging to ascertain whether a hedging strategy is appropriate. To sum up, therefore, the first step in the hedge decision is to work out a net exposed balances table and combine this information with an interest rate probability distribution to determine the risk exposure on a cash basis.

8.3 What Hedging Alternatives are Available and What Will They Cost?

If a company examines its risk exposure and concludes that it is unacceptably high it will consider various hedging strategies. The first possibility is simply to alter the mismatches in the balance sheet. A company might react to the mismatch shown in Figure 8.1 by moving to a

Principles of hedging in financial futures

Table 8.3. Probability of interest rate changes

Probability (Q2)	Rate (%)	Probability (Q3)	Rate (%)	Probability (Q4)	Rate (%)
0.1	9	0.1	10	0.3	10
0.2	8	0.1	9	0.3	9
0.4	7	0.6	8	0.2	8
0.2	6	0.1	7	0.1	7
0.1	5	0.1	6	0.1	6
Mean expected rate	7		8		8.6
Probability rate less than 9%	96.6%		78.5%		68.1%
Mean rate contingent on negative rate change	6.8		7.6		7.3

Table 8.4. Cash values of risk

	(Q2)	(Q3)	(Q4)
Net exposed balance	£1,000m	£1,000m	£1,500m
Probability rate < 9%	96.6%	78.5%	68.1%
Cash risk level	£106,260m	£58,875m	£40,860m

The cash risk level in dollars is found using the following formula:

Cash risk = Current rate − [Mean rate contingent in adverse rate change]

$$\times \frac{\text{Number of days exposure}}{360} \times \text{Probability of adverse rate change} \times \text{Net exposed balance}$$

matched book position, and thereby increase the amount of natural hedging. In reality it is unlikely that any major company will be able to run a fully matched book for any substantial period of time. However, moves to increase the amount of natural hedging should always be explored before considering more complex hedging strategies.

A second alternative is to lock in borrowing and/or lending rates through the forward–forward market. In a simple case where a bank is worried about increasing rates and would like to lock in the rate at which it will be able to borrow funds in three months' time, it could achieve this by lending for three months and borrowing for six months, ensuring that it will be able to borrow for three months in three months' time at the forward-forward rate. The use of the forward–forward market to lock in future borrowing or lending rates is often advantageous to banks because they operate on the favourable side of the bid–ask spread.

Nevertheless, the forward–forward market has two significant drawbacks. Firstly, the high spread between borrowing and investing interest

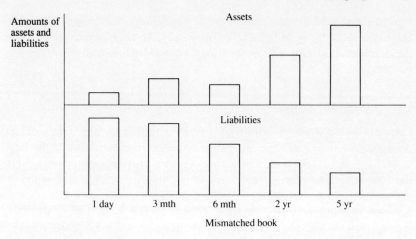

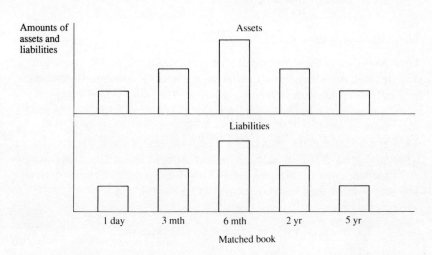

Figure 8.1 Matched and mis-matched book

rates could result in a high forward rate. Secondly, both the borrowing and lending transactions will appear on the balance sheet. For non-banks in particular, therefore, forward rate agreements or futures contracts would be more attractive.

8.4 Cross Hedging

Hedging one financial instrument with a futures contract on a different underlying instrument is known as cross hedging. The investor will

Principles of hedging in financial futures

typically hedge using a futures contract which has a close correlation with the instrument he is hedging. Not unusually, however, there may be no financial futures contract closely enough correlated with the cash instrument to warrant the hedge.

8.5 Correlation Analysis

Correlation analysis is concerned with determining the relationship between two time series, i.e. interest rates, exchange rates, etc. If the two series increase and decrease simultaneously they are positively correlated; if they move independently, they have zero correlation; and, if they move inversely they have negative correlation. The strength of correlation between two interest rates or price series is vital in determining whether futures written on one instrument can be used to hedge cash market exposure in another instrument.

8.6 Linear Regression

After establishing the existence of a reasonably strong and stable relationship through correlation analysis, the next stage is to examine the structure of the relationship with regression analysis. The most common regression technique is known as least squares analysis. With two variables the model constructs an equation relating one variable (the dependent variable) to another (the independent variable). The best way to show a simple linear regression relationship is in the form of a straight line with the dependent and independent variables represented on the Y and X axis respectively. The equation of such a straight line can be written as:

$$Y = a + b \cdot x$$

a = intercept on Y axis of the scatter diagram
b = slope of the regression line

Example 8.2 Calculating the regression equation
To ascertain the change in yield on short gilts which corresponds to a 1% change in the three month sterling deposit rate, we could construct a scatter diagram as shown in Figure 8.2 and then calculate a line of best fit using the above formula $y = a + b \cdot x$. The intercept on the Y axis in Figure 8.2 is equal to 6.74%. This indicates that the average premium on five year gilts over three months' sterling time deposits is 6.74%. The regression coefficient $b = 0.47$, indicating that a 1% change in the time deposit rate will generally be associated with a 0.47% change in the five year gilt yield:

$Y = 6.74 + 0.47 \ x$
$R^2 = 0.6641$

64

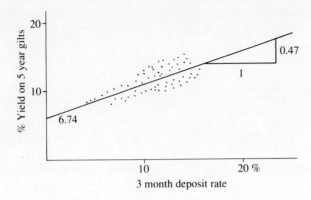

Figure 8.2 Change in yield on short gilts

From the regression equation above we can derive a value for R^2. This is the best known indicator of the success of a least squares fit. The R^2 figure measures the percentage of the change in the dependent or Y variable in the regression equation which has been caused by changes in the independent or X variable. Generally, the higher the R^2, the better fitted is the equation; R^2 must be between zero and 1 and, like the correlation coefficient, measures the linear relationship between two variables. Consequently, a value of $R^2 = 0$ implies a lack of linearity rather than a lack of association.

The importance of linear regression and correlation coefficients in hedge design is that the correlation coefficient is a measure of the average relative volatility of two financial instrument yields. For example, suppose we regressed six month Eurodollar rates on three month Eurodollar futures implied yields (a regression of rate changes on rate changes) and found a correlation coefficient of 0.95. This would imply that if three month Eurodollar rates rose by 100 basis points, six month Eurodollar rates would rise by 95 basis points. This ratio is obviously important in determining a hedging strategy. The hedge indicated by the above would clearly involve less three month, than six month Eurodollar futures (at face value) because the regression relationship indicates that six month Eurodollar rates move less than three month Eurodollar futures implied rates.

8.7 Deciding How Many Futures Contracts are Required for a Good Hedge (the hedge ratio)

Having chosen a suitable futures hedge vehicle highly correlated to the cash position and suitably liquid, the next step is to decide the number of futures

Principles of hedging in financial futures

Table 8.5. Equivalent values

	0.01% of £250,000 (£)	0.01% of $1,000,000 ($)
One year	25.00	100.00
9 months	18.75	75.00
6 months	12.50	50.00
3 months	6.25	25.00
1 month	2.08	8.33

contracts necessary to produce a good hedge. This decision involves four basic stages.

1. Face value of the contracts

Consideration must be given to the ratio of the cash amount to be hedged, to the face value of the underlying contracts. *Ceteris paribus*, you would consider hedging £5,000,000 of sterling CDs with 20 sterling interest rate futures of £250,000 face value. Similarly, you would hedge a $1,000,000 corporate bond position with 10 T-bond futures contracts of $100,000 face value, and so on.

2. Money equivalency

The change in price of a futures contract or a cash instrument for a given interest rate change obviously varies according to the maturity of the instrument. Table 8.5 shows the equivalent value of an interest change of 0.01% for typical contract sizes of £250,000 and $1,000,000. The price change of a six month instrument induced by a 1% change in interest rates will be double that of a three month instrument. This has implications for the hedge. To hedge $1,000,000 of a six month cash instrument will, *ceteris paribus*, require $2,000,000 of a three month financial futures contract. Similarly, to hedge $1,000,000 of a one month cash instrument would only require $333,000 of the same three month futures contract. The aim here is to hedge money equivalency.

3. Correlation coefficients

Correlation has already been used as a measure of the linear relationship of the basis between a cash instrument and a given change in the futures instrument (and vice versa). To determine the number of future contracts necessary to provide a good hedge we can use the following formula which applies the correlation coefficients of the cash and futures contracts to their respective face values and money equivalences:

> Number of contracts required = Face value of cash position/Face value of futures contracts × Money equivalency × Regression coefficient

This formula only applies to short term futures contracts priced on an index basis. Determining hedge quantities in long term contracts, i.e. gilts and T-bond futures, requires a different approach (see below).

Example 8.3 Calculating the hedge

Suppose a company wishes to hedge a $20,000,000 position in six month commercial paper. Two futures contracts appear to offer sufficient liquidity: International Monetary Market (IMM) 90 day T-bills and IMM 90-day certificates of deposit. The following correlation coefficients have been derived:

90 day T-bills future $R = 0.967$ (standard contract size $1,000,000)
90 day certificates of deposit $R = 0.97$ (standard contract size $1,000,000)

The company would choose to hedge with CD futures because of the higher correlation and calculate the number of contracts necessary to hedge the position by using the following formula:

$$\text{No. of contracts required} = \frac{\$20,000,000}{\$1,000,000} \times \frac{\$50 \ (6 \ \text{month})}{\$25 \ (3 \ \text{month})} \times 0.97$$
$$= 38.8$$

Approximately 39 CD futures contracts are therefore required for the hedge.

4. *Conversion or price factors*

There is another feature of relative price movements that influences the effectiveness of a hedge. This applies to those contracts where a variety of different instruments are deliverable (e.g. gilt futures) and the futures price applies to one long term standardised contract.

Money equivalency does not apply to these long term contracts, which are typically priced on a discount basis. The price of the particular cash instrument being hedged can respond differently to an interest rate change than the price of the standardised futures contract being used to hedge it. Accordingly, hedgers do not always choose to hedge a specific cash position with an equal valued futures position. Nevertheless, provided arbitrage pressures exist in the market, the relationship between individual cash

Principles of hedging in financial futures

prices and the price of the standard gilt should be constant during the life of the contract. A conversion factor will therefore be applied in deciding how many futures contracts are necessary to hedge:

No. of contracts required

$$= \frac{\text{Face value of cash position}}{\text{Face value of futures contract}} \times \text{Conversion factor}$$

Example 8.4 Price factor hedging
A portfolio manager holds a portfolio of $15,000,000 face value of $7\frac{5}{8}$% 15 March 2002 T-bonds on 1 February 1988. Suppose the price factor of a $7\frac{5}{8}$% bond with 14 years to maturity is 0.9734.

$$\text{No. of contracts required} = \frac{\$15,000,000}{\$100,000} \times 0.9734$$

Therefore, approximately 146 $7\frac{5}{8}$% future bonds will be necessary to hedge the position. *Note:* the actual construction of conversion prices is discussed later.

The assumption implicit in the use of conversion factors is that a change in interest rates will affect gilts, or T-bonds, of different maturities and coupon yields, in exactly the manner dictated by the conversion factors. In reality, this is not the case and, therefore, two other analytical techniques can be used: perturbation analysis and duration analysis. These are explained later in Chapters 12 and 13 covering US T-bond futures and gilt futures.

8.8 The Hedge Management Process

Once the decision to hedge has been implemented, hedge management then becomes vital. Essentially, it involves the following three distinct processes:

1. hedge monitoring;
2. hedge adjustment;
3. hedge evaluation.

1. *Hedge monitoring*

In order to monitor the hedged position it is essential that the following information is available and up-to-date.

(a) *Cash position:* in addition to the original risk exposure levels that currently exist, the net opportunity or current realised loss or gain to the cash position must also be identified.
(b) *Futures position:* the size and profit (or loss) to the futures position

68

must be clearly identified. The total amount of margin currently assigned to the position should be known and any net margin financing costs should be projected for appropriate periods.

(c)   *Basis movements:* profit and losses to the futures position should be sub-divided into those due to overall interest rate movements and those due to basis changes.

(d)   *Financing requirements:* the extent of financial resources used to date for margin payments should be known, to determine the viability and adequacy of resources necessary for continuation of the hedge.

(e)   *Fulfilment of forecasts:* original forecasts for interest rates, exchange rates and basis should be compared with the current situation and any necessary adjustments implemented.

(f)   *Regression and correlation:* correlation and regression data used in designing the hedge strategy should be compared with the situation to date, to ascertain its appropriateness.

2.   *Hedge adjustment*

The hedge monitoring process provides most of the information necessary to adjust the hedge throughout its life. Various reasons for hedge adjustment are identifiable:

(a)   *Alterations in risk exposure:* if the cash market sums change because cash flows are unexpectedly high (or unexpectedly low) the size of the hedge will change correspondingly. This may involve realising losses on contracts no longer required for a hedge function.

(b)   *Alterations in risk preferences:* if management changes or the objectives of the company alter, previous hedging strategies may not be appropriate.

(c)   *Interest rate projections:* a forward-looking probability distribution of interest rates is vital in determining risk exposure and an effective hedge strategy. Changes in interest rate forecasts can therefore lead to major changes in the hedging strategy.

(d)   *Increasing liquidity:* nearby contracts may be switched into more distant contracts during the life of the hedge as liquidity in those contracts improves.

(e)   *Up-to-date hedge ratio components:* changes in correlation coefficients may affect the required number of contracts necessary to match a particular cash position.

3.   *Hedge evaluation*

Basically, the objective in managing the hedged position is to optimise its efficiency as determined by the following:

$$\text{Hedge efficiency} = \frac{\text{Gain (loss) on futures position}}{\text{Gain (loss) on cash position}}$$

The two main inputs into hedge efficiency are, firstly, the size of the basis changes and secondly, the quality of the components of the hedge ratio, i.e. correlation results and conversion factors.

8.9 Conclusion

In the next chapter we will examine the technicalities and applications of certain futures contracts, applying the principles already described. Although LIFFE now has the most comprehensive range of financial futures and option products of any exchange in the world, emphasis will be placed upon the LIFFE interest rate, currency, gilt and T-bond futures contracts.

CHAPTER 9

Short-term interest rate futures

9.1 Introduction

During the 1970s and early 1980s interest rates were particularly volatile and the need for some form of interest rate protection became apparent. This gave rise to the development of interest rate futures and interest rate option contracts being traded on the financial futures markets.

9.2 Interest Rate Futures

An interest rate futures contract fixes the effective interest rate for borrowing or lending funds at a specific date in the future. A company anticipating losses from a decrease in interest rates, for instance, could therefore take up a futures position that would provide gains from decreasing interest rates. Such a position could arise where a company is anticipating receipt of funds in, say, fifty days time and is then hoping to invest for three months at current levels of interest rates (see Example 9.1). Conversely, where a company is anticipating an increase in interest rates and is contemplating a short-term loan in the near future, a futures position can be taken that will apply present-day interest rates to the eventual loan.

9.3 Standardisation

Trading in short-term interest rate futures on LIFFE takes place in either sterling or Eurodollars. The standard unit of trading for sterling contracts is £500,000 and for Eurodollars $US1,000,000. Delivery occurs in either March, June, September or December, with the actual delivery day taking place on the first business day after the last trading day. For sterling interest rate futures the last trading day is the third Wednesday of the delivery month and for Eurodollar futures it is two business days prior to the third Wednesday of the delivery month. Both types of contract are quoted on the exchange at 100.00 minus an annualised rate of interest and have a tick size of 0.01 (i.e. £12.50 sterling contracts and $US25.00 Eurodollar contracts).

Short-term interest rate futures

The initial margin is £500 and $US750 respectively, with both contracts being eventually settled in cash, rather than a deposit, to compensate any deviation of realised rates from guaranteed rates.

The majority of short-term interest rate futures contracts are closed out prior to maturity. When closing out occurs, hedgers would have typically received or paid a variation margin to offset movement in interest rates. Thus a potential investor, having to accept less because of decreased interest rates, should have received, at or prior to maturity, a sum of money to compensate for the lower interest rate receipts.

9.4 Pricing of Eurodollar Futures

The usual basis for estimating the fair price of a short-term LIFFE Eurodollar futures contract is the determination of whether an arbitrage opportunity exists between the futures market and the cash market.

> **Example 9.1 Calculating a Eurodollar futures price**
>
> Taking the example of a Eurodollar contract for delivery on 20 December, suppose the current spot date is 30 October. The price would be calculated as follows:
>
>
> 50 day Eurodollar interest rate 30 October midpoint = 10%
> 140 day Eurodollar interest rate 30 October midpoint = 10.5%
>
> This information enables us to calculate the forward–forward price for the period 20 December–20 March:
>
> $$\text{90 day forward–forward} = \left\{ \left[\frac{1 + (0.105 \times (140/360))}{1 + (0.10 \times (50/360))} \right] - 1 \right\} \times \frac{360}{90}$$
>
> $$= 0.1063 \ (10.63\%)$$
>
> Since this is the mid point rate (half-way between the bid and offer rates), LIBOR (London Inter-bank Offered Rate) is obtained by adding $\frac{1}{16}$% (half the usual $\frac{1}{8}$% bid–offer spread).
>
> Equivalent LIBOR rate = 10.63% + 0.0625%
>   = 10.69%
>
> Since the Eurodollar futures price is [100 − annualised interest rate (LIBOR in this example)], the equivalent fair futures price for 20 December delivery is

$(100 - 10.69) = 89.31$

This price is an indices used to calculate the gains and losses from futures trading, rather than representing money payable for contracts.

9.5 Value Basis and Simple Basis

The difference between this indices or theoretical futures price and the actual December futures price is termed the value basis and measures how undervalued or overvalued the futures contract is relative to the cash market. If the value basis is very positive then opportunities may exist for arbitrage or spread trading.

It is important to distinguish between value basis and simple basis. Simple basis is just the difference between the futures price implied by the current three month interest rate and the actual futures price. In the preceding example, for instance, if the spot three month LIBOR rate on 30 October had been 10.25%, this would have implied an equivalent futures price of 89.75.

Therefore, if December actual futures price = 89.25
Basis = 89.75 − 89.25 = 50 basis points (0.5%)
Value basis = 89.31 − 89.25 = 6 basis points (0.06%)

At delivery both basis and value basis will be zero (see Figure 9.1). Similarly, prior to delivery arbitrage should keep the value basis small; however, over the period of the contract, basis will reflect the shape of the cash market yield curve which can be both large and volatile.

Figure 9.1 Basis convergence

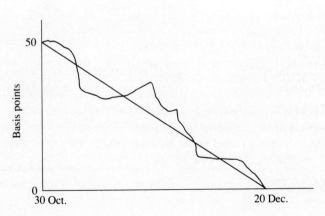

Short-term interest rate futures

Example 9.2 Interest rate hedging using the Eurodollar futures market

On 1 August suppose that a company borrows $1,000,000 on the Eurodollar market for three months at 8% per annum. The borrowing is scheduled to be rolled over on 1 November. Anticipating that rates may have risen by then, the company sells a December, $1 million Eurodollar three month futures contract at a price of 91.00. This enables the company to lock into currently available interest rates, specifically 9%, for the three months beginning in December. (This happens to be one percentage point above the current rate on the spot market.)

By 1 November when the firm rolls over the $1,000,000 loan, the current rate of interest has risen to 10%. The company will roll over its borrowing at this rate but will also buy a December three month Eurodollar futures contract at a price (assuming the interest rate on the futures contract has remained at one percentage point above the spot rate) of 89.00. This second futures transaction is called 'closing out' the previous position in the market. The two futures deals together yield a profit of $5,000 (2% of $1,000,000 for three months), exactly offsetting the extra cost incurred in the spot market because of the rise in interest rates. In other words, the net cost at which the borrowing is being rolled over is 10%. This hedge can be shown in terms of the company's activities in both the cash market and the futures market:

Cash Market

On 1 August the company borrows $1,000,000 at a current spot rate of 8% per annum, with the intention of rolling it over in three months time on 1 November. When the loan is eventually rolled over the new spot interest rate is 10% per annum, which will incur an extra cost of $5,000 for the company, i.e.:

$$\frac{2\% \times 1,000,000}{4}$$

Futures Market

Anticipating that interest rates might increase, the company could arrange to sell a $1,000,000 December three month Eurodollar futures contract at a price of 91.00 (rate = 9%) on 1 August. In the event of spot interest rates rising, the company will 'close out' the previous position on the futures market by buying a $1,000,000 December three month Eurodollar futures contract at the new price of 89.00 (rate = 11%). The net gain from the two futures deal will be $5,000, i.e.:

$$\frac{2\% \times 1,000,000}{4}$$

74

Taking the basis forecast into account

In this example, the hedge worked perfectly – the gain on the futures was exactly equal to the extra interest incurred and achieved a net borrowing cost of 8% per annum. If interest rates had fallen, the hedger's loss on his futures position would have been matched by lower interest payments and his net borrowing cost would still have been 8% per annum. However, such perfect matching is unusual as futures prices do not typically move exactly in line with cash market rates.

9.6 Basis Change

We have already suggested that the major reason why perfect hedges do not materialise in practice is that basis (difference between the cash and futures prices) can vary considerably over time. If the basis changes adversely during the life of a hedge, then a part of the offsetting gain on the futures contract can be eliminated, making the hedge imperfect.

The perfect short hedge (described above) illustrates this. Consider what would have happened if the three month Eurodollar futures price on 1 November had been 89.40, i.e. if the difference between the cash and futures price had started to converge as the delivery month approached. This represents an implicit basis change from 100 $(9\% - 8\%)$ basis points on 1 August to 60 $(10.6\% - 10\%)$ basis points on 1 November. The impact on the futures gain would be substantial, reducing it from 200 to 160 ticks per contract. The cash gain would therefore be reduced from \$5,000 to $160 \times \$25 = \$4,000$. Consequently, the futures gain would only cover 80% of the cash market loss, by no means a perfect hedge. If basis had moved in the opposite direction, there would have been a wind-fall gain on the futures side of the hedge.

9.7 Cross Hedging

Hedging a financial instrument with a futures contract on a different underlying instrument is known as cross hedging. It exposes the hedger to greater basis risk because there is less likelihood that interest rates on different financial instruments will move exactly together. In general, the investor should choose to hedge a cash instrument using a futures contract which suggests the best correlation.

9.8 Taking the Basis Forecast into Account

A basis hedging approach can be used to reduce the size of the hedge. Take the following example.

Short-term interest rate futures

Example 9.3 Basis Hedging

Suppose a hedger wishes to hedge a risk exposure of a $10,000,000 six month term loan on 30 May. The relevant regression coefficient with three month June Eurodollar futures is 0.98. The hedger is concerned that rates will fall and thus endeavours to create a short hedge. The current six month Eurodollar rate is $8\frac{1}{2}\%$, the current three month rate is $8\frac{1}{4}\%$ and the current June Eurodollar futures price is 92.50.

Step 1

Work out the numbers of contracts required:

$$\text{No. of contracts} = \frac{10,000,000}{1,000,000} \times \frac{\$50}{\$25} \times 0.98 \approx 20$$

Step 2

The hedger forecasts that by 30 May the cash three month Eurodollar rate to June futures implied rate will decline from 75 to 15 basis points. If this occurs, the profit to the futures position, assuming no cash market change, is:

Gains from basis = 60 (decline in basis points) × 20 (No. of contracts) × $25 = $30,000

Step 3

Combine the estimated extra profit of $30,000 with the interest rate forecast and reduce the required number of contracts. If we assume that the forecast is for a maximum reduction in interest rates of 2%, the required futures gain to hedge is calculated as follows:

$$\text{Gain from rate change} = \$10,000,000 \times 0.02 \times \frac{\$25}{\$50} = \$100,000$$

$$\text{Gain per contract from basis change} = \$1,500 \left(\text{i.e. } \frac{\$30,000}{20} \right)$$

$$\text{Gain per contract from 2\% rate change} = \$5,000 \left(\text{i.e. } \frac{\$100,000}{20} \right)$$

$$\text{No. of contracts} \approx 16 \left(\frac{100,000}{6,500} \right)$$

The forecast profit per contract from the expected decline is used to reduce the number of contracts needed for a full hedge.

9.9 Three Month Sterling Interest Rate Futures Contracts

A sterling futures contract fixes the effective interest rate for borrowing or lending three month sterling funds at a specific date in the future. The mechanics of margining and delivery are similar to those explained for Eurodollar interest rate futures.

The price calculation is exactly the same as for Eurodollar futures, but sterling interest rates are used instead. We would, therefore, calculate the forward–forward rate from the two given periods (see Example 9.1) and add half the usual $\frac{1}{8}\%$ spread and deduct from 100 to arrive at the price indices:

i.e. 90 day forward–forward $\quad = 0.9020\% \ (9.02\%)$
Equivalent LIBOR rate $\quad = 9.020\% + 0.0625\%$
$\quad = 9.08\%$
Price $= (100 - 9.08) = 90.92$

9.10 Uses of Three Month Sterling Futures

Example 9.4

Suppose a company treasurer decides to hedge his next rollover of £5,000,000 three month loan due on 17 June. The loan is at a spread of 0.5% above LIBOR. The problem confronting the company treasurer is to anticipate correctly the likely net borrowing rate for 20 June and then to adopt a hedging strategy that will guarantee this rate. The current rates and prices are as below:

6 March
Three month LIBOR $\quad\quad\quad\quad\quad\quad\quad\quad\quad\quad 8\frac{7}{8}\%$
LIFFE three month sterling June $\quad\quad\quad\quad\quad 91.00$

June Futures delivery date $\quad\quad\quad\quad\quad\quad\quad$ 16 June
Last trading day $\quad\quad\quad\quad\quad\quad\quad\quad\quad\quad\quad$ 15 June

The interest rate implied by the futures contract:
3 month LIBOR on 15 June is 9% [(100.00 − 9.00) = 91.00]
Actual rate with spread of 0.5% = 9.5%
The compensating variation margin will be 91.00 − EDSP

The exchange delivery selling price (EDSP) is determined by current rates in the cash market. For instance, if the annualised interest rate decreased from 9% on 6 March to 8.99% the following day, the contract price would similarly change from 91.00 to 91.01. Under the terms of the futures contract acquired on 6 March the hedger would be guaranteed a receipt of 2.25% × £500,000 per contract, i.e. £11,250 over a three month period commencing on 16 June (third Thursday in June). However, a reduction in interest rates in accordance with the above would mean that if the hedger had acquired the contract on 7 March, he would only be guaranteed 2.2475% (8.99/4) × £500,000 per contract, i.e. £11,237.50, a reduction of £12.50 in the guaranteed sum, equivalent to one tick. The hedger thus has the option of either selling the contract and receiving the value of one tick, or in the absence of closing out the contract, having the £12.50 paid to him as variation margin.

The Hedge

The treasurer will contract to sell 10 three month sterling contracts at 91.00 on 6 March (unit of trading is £500,000 – hence, 10 contracts cover £5,000,000).

Suppose that on 15 June, three month LIBOR is $9\frac{3}{8}\%$ and the treasurer must borrow funds at

$$9\frac{3}{8}\% + \frac{1}{2}\% = 9\frac{7}{8}\%$$

At this time the LIFFE June three month sterling futures contract is priced at 90.63, which suggest a futures profit of

$$(91.00 - 90.63) \times £12.50 \times 10 = £4,625$$

(Note: $91.00 - 90.63 = 37$ ticks at £12.50 each × 10 = £4,625.) The net borrowing rate implicit in this hedge is therefore:

$$\frac{5,000,000 \times (0.09875 \times \frac{3}{12}) - 4,625}{5,000,000} \times 4$$

$$= 9.5\%$$

(as anticipated) despite the increase in cash interest rates.

9.11 Considerations When Choosing a Futures Contract For Hedging

1. Normally choose to hedge using the futures contract most closely correlated with the cash position.
2. Correlation can change through time and past correlations may not necessarily be good predictors of future correlation.
3. Ensure that the chosen futures contract possesses sufficient liquidity to create a hedge in sufficient volume.
4. Always compare historical variation in basis with historical variation in rates. A badly correlated hedge may be better than none at all.
5. Calculate the transaction and execution costs for the hedge that looks most suitable.

9.12 Using Interest Rate Futures to Offer Fixed Rate Funds

The preceding examples of interest rate hedging have been basic examples of hedging typically adopted by corporate treasurers. Let us now look at an example from the view point of a lending bank. A major opportunity is provided by the futures market to enable banks to offer fixed rate loans to customers.

Example 9.5 Offering fixed rate funds

A typical example might be where a bank intends to lend £5,000,000 at a fixed rate for one year. Suppose the loan is to be made on 10 March and repaid in full on 10 March the following year, with interest being paid quarterly. The intention is to price the loan at a spread of 100 basis points over the sterling three month interbank rate. The current range of prices and yields applicable on 10 March are as shown in Table 9.1. The first step is to determine the price that can be offered to the customer. This is done by combining the four rates quoted in the table into an equivalent annual yield. The customer will then be quoted this rate plus 100 basis points. As we are directly comparing this with a floating rate loan, the equivalent annual rate is the arithmetic average of the cash rate and the three implied futures rates, i.e. 9.56%. The loan will be quoted at 10.56% (9.56% + 100 basis points).

Step One: 10 March

1. Borrow sterling interbank funds for 92 days at 9%
   Total cost = £5,000,000 × 0.09 × $\frac{92}{365}$ = £113,424.66
   (sterling interest is calculated on a 365 day basis)
2. Sell 10 June sterling time deposit futures at 90.50
   Sell 10 September futures at 90.25
   Sell 10 December futures at 90.00

Step Two: 10 June

1. Borrow sterling interbank funds for 92 days at 10%
   Total cost = £5,000,000 × 0.10 × $\frac{92}{365}$ = £126,027.40
2. Buy 10 sterling deposit futures at 89.90
   Futures gain = 60 (90.50 − 89.90) × 10 × £12.50 = £7,500
   Effective borrowing rate 10 June–10 September

$$= \left(\frac{126,027.40 - 7,500}{5,000,000}\right) \times \frac{365}{92} = 9.40\%$$

Step Three: 10 September

1. Borrow sterling interbank for 91 days at 9.9%

$$\text{Total cost} = £5,000,000 \times 0.099 \times \frac{91}{365} = £123,410.96$$

79

Short-term interest rate futures

Table 9.1. Sample cash and futures prices

Cash 3 month interbank		June sterling deposit future	September future	December future
Price		90.50	90.25	90.00
Rate	9.00	9.50	9.75	10.00

2. Buy 10 September futures at 90.06

Futures gain $= 19\ (90.25 - 90.06) \times 10 \times £12.50 = £2{,}375$

3. Effective borrowing rate 10 September–10 December

$$= \left(\frac{123{,}410.96 - 2{,}375}{5{,}000{,}000}\right) \times \frac{365}{91} = 9.71\%$$

Step Four: 10 December

1. Borrow sterling interbank for 90 days at 8.8%

$$\text{Total cost} = £5{,}000{,}000 \times 0.088 \times \frac{90}{365} = £108{,}493.15$$

2. Buy 10 December futures at 91.23

Futures loss $= 123\ (90.00 - 91.23) \times 10 \times £12.50 = £15{,}375$

3. Effective borrowing rate 10 December–10 March

$$= \left(\frac{108{,}493.15 + 15{,}375}{5{,}000{,}000}\right) \times \frac{365}{90} = 10.05\%$$

Actual hedged borrowing cost for the bank

$$= \left(9 \times \frac{92}{365}\right) + \left(9.40 \times \frac{92}{365}\right) + \left(9.71 \times \frac{91}{365}\right) + \left(10.05 \times \frac{90}{365}\right)$$

$$= 9.54\%$$

This compares favourably with our original estimated borrowing cost of 9.56%. The realised spread on the loan is 102 basis points; however, variation margins will have been paid on the futures positions. The actual amount of variation margin will depend upon the daily price movements in the futures prices but this can be taken into account by making some simple assumptions about profits and losses which are assumed to have occurred continuously throughout the period. Similarly, both initial and variation margins are assumed to have been financed or to have earned interest at the average interbank rate for the three month period concerned.

Margin Costs

(a)   10 June contracts. Initial margin $= 10 + £500 = -£5,000$.
Average variation margin $= £7,500/2 = £3,750$
Margin of £1,250 $(-£5,000 + £3,750)$ to be financed at a rate equal
to $(9 + 10)/2 = 9\frac{1}{2}\%$
Margin cost $= £1,250 \times 0.095 \times 92/365 = £29.93$

(b)   10 September contracts. Initial margin $= -£5,000$
Average variation margin $= £2,375/2 = £1,187.50$.
Margin of £3,812.50 to be financed at a rate equal to
$(9 + 10 + 9.9)/3 = 9\frac{19}{30}\%$
Margin cost $= 3812.50 \times 0.0963 \times (\frac{92+92}{365}) = £185.14$

(c)   20 December. Initial margin $= -£5,000$
Average variation margin $= -£15,375/2 = -£7,687.50$
Margin of £7,687.50 to be financed at a rate equal to
$(9 + 10 + 9.9 + 8.8)/4 = 9.425\%$
Margin cost $= £7,687.50 \times 0.09425 \times 275/365 = £545.89$

Combining these margin costs with the figures estimated earlier gives a net
borrowing rate as follows:

$$(9 \times 92/365) + (9.41 \times 92/365) + (9.72 \times 92/365) + (10.09 \times 90/365)$$
$$= 9.58\%$$

This is two basis points higher than the original estimate, suggesting that
when banks offer fixed rate loans they do need to consider margin costs
carefully when determining the cost of fixed funds obtained via futures
market hedging. The use of financial futures markets in enabling banks to
offer fixed rate loans to customers has even further potential. Several banks
have introduced schemes whereby fixed rate funds are made available to
customers at specific dates in the future. These schemes broadly fall into
the two following categories:

1.   The customer undertakes to borrow a fixed sum at a fixed rate specified
in the future. This is a classic hedging strategy for the customer who
consequently foregoes the opportunity of benefiting from lower
interest rates.
2.   The bank offers to lend the customer funds at some specified future date
at market rates applicable when the funds are drawn. In addition, the
bank guarantees that the rate will not be higher than a certain level. In
this case, therefore, the customer retains the opportunity of benefiting
from lower interest rates.

9.13   Which Rates for the Customer?

In providing these facilities the bank must first decide which fixed interest will be offered to the customer. There are several alternatives, as follows.

(a)   current market rates prevailing in the cash market;
(b)   interest rates embedded in current futures prices;
(c)   interest rates implicit in the forward–forward market;
(d)   interest rates determined at the discretion of the borrower.

It is possible for a bank to be very flexible and to offer fixed rates at various future dates and for loans of different maturities. The provision of such flexible fixed rates necessitates conventional hedging of the type described earlier, and would expose either the borrower or lender to basis risk, i.e. the risk that interest rates in the cash market will not move exactly in line with futures prices. Since bank customers are not usually willing to assume this risk, the bank typically does and charges an appropriate spread.

Banks can also avoid basis risk by locking into a future date directly through the futures market or the forward–forward market. It is relatively easy for banks with direct access to the interbank market to lock in borrowing and lending rates through the forward–forward market. This is undoubtedly the easiest way to offer fixed rate money at a future date and, as the bank will be on the right side of the bid-offer spread, is probably the most profitable.

For institutions with restricted access to the forward–forward interbank market, there remains the possibility of offering fixed rate funds at a spread over the rates prevailing in the futures market. However, to avoid basis risk, funds would need to be offered only for three month periods commencing on the delivery dates of the relevant short term interest rate futures contracts. This would put considerable restrictions on the financing alternatives offered to customers.

CHAPTER 10

Interest rate options

10.1 Introduction

Prior to 1973 and the opening of the Chicago Board Options Exchange (CBOE), options in both stocks and commodities were traded on an over-the-counter basis. However, subsequent to the opening of CBOE and the foundation of the Options Clearing Corporation to guarantee performance on stock option contracts, there was a vast increase in the volume of financial options trading in the United States and in the number of underlying assets, such as currencies, stock indices and Treasury bonds.

Interest rate options are traded on exchanges in the United States (the Chicago Board Options Exchange (cash), the American Stock Exchange (cash), the Chicago Board of Trade (futures), the Chicago Mercantile Exchange (futures)); Europe (the London Stock Exchange (cash) and the London International Financial Futures Exchange (futures)); and Australia (the Sydney Futures Exchange (futures)).

An option confers the right to borrow (or lend) at a specific rate of interest for a particular period of time, commencing either immediately or at a predetermined time in the future. A hedger, however, is not obliged to borrow (or lend) at that rate. For instance, a company wishing to borrow £5 million at some time in the future could contract to buy an option at a prespecified exercise (strike) rate of interest and therefore safeguard against the risk of rising interest rates. If interest rates increased beyond that specified in the option, the option would be exercised and the counterparty (the writer of the option) would provide a £5,000,000 loan at the prespecified rate of interest. However, if interest rates declined below the prespecified rate, then the borrower would choose not to exercise the option and borrow at the more favourable current market rates.

In return, the writer of the option would be paid a premium by the buyer. The size of this premium is determined by the expected volatility of interest rates and the direction of the option. The relationship of the exercise rate to current rates is also an important determinant of premium size. The further-in-money an option is (i.e. exercise rates below current market rates) the

83

greater will be its intrinsic value (i.e. the gain from immediate exercise of the option) and the higher premiums will be. Conversely, if the option is out-of-the-money (i.e. exercise rate in excess of current market rates) there will be no intrinsic value and the premium value will be relatively smaller, reflecting solely the time value element.

The buyer of an option either to borrow or lend funds) can therefore limit his potential for loss (i.e. downside risk) and yet maintain an unlimited potential for gain (i.e. upside risk). For instance, in our above example, if current interest rates were less than the prespecified rates in the option, the buyer would not exercise the option. He would borrow at current interest rates and pay the premium to the writer of the option. Downside risk is, therefore, limited to the size of the premium payable and upside potential is unlimited being equal to the difference between the rate specified in the option and current interest rates, less the premium payable. If interest rates had increased, however, the buyer would have exercised the option. The upside potential would have been unlimited, being determined by the difference between current market rates and the rates specified in the option, less the premium payable.

The writer of an option has a limited potential for gain determined by the size of the premium. The potential for loss, however, is unlimited being determined by the difference between current market rates and the rate specified in the option. The effect of this can be mitigated to some extent by the writer of the option compensating the buyer for any interest rate deviation from that specified in the option.

10.2   Standardisation

Apart from OTC (over-the-counter) interest rate options, available mainly from banks, traded options are obtainable on LIFFE and the London Stock Exchange. On LIFFE the unit of trading is either one long gilt futures contract, one Treasury bond contract, one Eurodollar futures contract or one three month sterling futures contract. Delivery is either March, June, September or December, with exercise taking place on any business day. Quotations for premiums are in multiples of 0.01% for Eurodollar and three month sterling futures contracts and $\frac{1}{64}$ for long gilts and Treasury bond contracts. Each of these amounts reflects the tick sizes for each of the contracts.

10.3   Eurodollar Option Contracts

The following sections concentrate upon three month Eurodollar future options but the same basic principles apply to all the various option instruments currently available. Essentially, a Eurodollar option contract is the right to buy (call) or sell (put) a Eurodollar futures contract at a specific price (the exercise price) on or before a specific date in the future (the expiration date). Traded options give the buyer a choice of exercise price which on LIFFE are available at 50 basis (0.50%) intervals, i.e. 11, 10.5 and 10%.

Call Option Example

15 September prices

> December Eurodollars 90.00 call = 0.75
> December Eurodollars futures = 90.50

The investor who buys this call option has bought the right between 15 September and December to buy a December Eurodollar futures contract at an effective price of 90.00 (the price of a Eurodollar futures contract is equal to 100 – the annualised futures interest rate). The cost of this right (premium) is $1,875 (i.e. 75 basis points $\times$ $25).

The call option buyer is looking to guarantee a maximum futures price and therefore a minimum rate of interest at which to deposit dollars while retaining the right to invest at higher rates.

Put Option Example

Suppose the futures and option prices for 15 September are as follows:

> December Eurodollar 90.00 put = 0.25
> December Eurodollar futures = 90.50

The investor who buys this put option has the right between 15 September and December to sell a December Eurodollar futures contract at an effective price of 90.00. The cost of this right is $625 (25 basis points $\times$ $25).

The put option buyer is looking to secure a maximum ceiling to interest payable on a loan, by guaranteeing a minimum selling price of futures contracts, while retaining the right to borrow elsewhere at cheaper rates if available.

10.4 Profit and Loss Profiles of Eurodollar Options

Figure 10.1 shows the profit and loss profiles of a buyer and seller of a Eurodollar call option. Both options have an exercise price of 90.00 and a premium payable of 0.50. The buyer of a call option has the potential for unlimited profit if prices increase beyond 90.50 equal to the difference between the exercise price and the market price, less the premium payable of 0.50. At futures prices below 90.00, the call option shows a loss equal to

Interest rate options

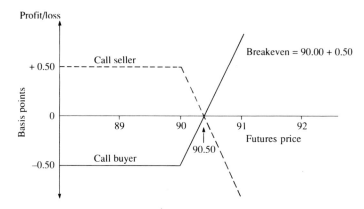

Figure 10.1 Profit and loss profiles on a Eurodollar call

0.50 (i.e. the premium payable). The option holder would not exercise the right to buy at 90.00 and would incur a loss equivalent to the premium payable.

The seller of a call option has the potential to make a profit equal to the premium payable, i.e. 0.50. However, as prices increase beyond 90.50, i.e. exercise price less premium, the potential for loss is unlimited being equal to the current market price less the exercise price.

Figure 10.2 shows the profit and loss profiles of a buyer and seller of a Eurodollar put option. The same principles as outlined for call options apply but in the opposite way.

Figure 10.2 Profit and loss profiles on a Eurodollar put

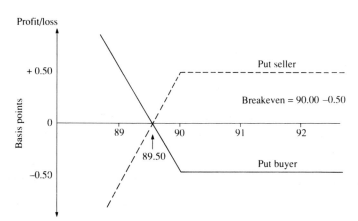

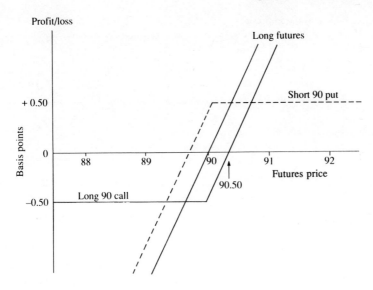

Figure 10.3 Comparing options and futures contracts

10.5 Options and Futures

The long Eurodollar call option position shown in Figure 10.3 behaves like a long Eurodollar futures contract with a guaranteed stop-loss order, but with an effective purchase price 0.50 (i.e. the premium payable) above the current futures price. The short Eurodollar put position behaves like a long Eurodollars futures contract with a guaranteed profit taking order and an effective purchase price 0.50 below the current futures price. Many different profit and loss profiles can be generated by being long and/or short of the underlying futures contract and the futures option on a similar basis to that seen with currency options.

The pricing of option contracts is similar to currency option contracts – consisting of intrinsic value and time value, with volatility (as before) being the crucial factor. The volatility of Eurodollar futures prices, or interest rates, is the only non-directly observable variable in most option valuation models. Given the extreme sensitivity of Eurodollar option premiums to volatility, the accurate measurement and/or prediction of futures price, or interest rate volatility, is crucial to option traders and hedgers.

The other major element (as before) associated with option valuation models is the delta. The delta of a Eurodollar option is simply the proportional amount that the Eurodollar option premium will change for a given Eurodollar price change. This is a very important concept in risk

87

Interest rate options

Table 10.1. Sample put option prices

Exercise price	Premium (%)	Futures price
80.00	0.21	88.26
88.50	0.44	
89.00	0.78	

Table 10.2. Guaranteed and breakeven rates

	Best guaranteed rate (%) (i.e. max. borrowing rate)	Breakeven rate (%)
Futures (88.26)	11.74	11.74
88.00 Put	12.21	11.53(11.74 − 0.21)
88.50 Put	11.94	11.30(11.74 − 0.44)
89.00 Put	11.78	10.96(11.74 − 0.78)

exposure. An option with a low delta is less risky in dollar terms than an option with a high delta. Deltas also play a major role in assessing the short term sensitivity of options positions to movements in futures prices and in the design of options hedges.

10.6   Hedging with Eurodollar Options

In contrast to a futures hedge which fixes a specific interest rate, an options hedge is similar to the purchase of interest rate insurance. For the price of the option (the insurance premium) the buyer is protected (insured) against an adverse movement in interest rates while preserving the benefits of a favourable movement in rates. Different options will provide different types of insurance. Consider the set of premiums shown in Table 10.1, which gives rise to the information given in Table 10.2. This illustrates the major features of options hedging: firstly, hedging with different options allows the hedger a choice of different hedge costs and different guaranteed borrowing rates. The hedger can decide which level of risk to accept and which insurance premium to pay. Secondly, the best guaranteed rate with an options hedge is always less than the interest rate that can be guaranteed with the futures hedge. Finally, with an option hedge, there is always a certain interest rate at which the cost of borrowing will be less than with a futures hedge (moving past the breakeven rate).

Each type of hedge will be suitable for a different type of exposure. If the future cash position is certain, the best hedge will typically involve use of the futures market. If the cash flow is less certain, the options hedge will be less risky and is likely to be preferred. An options hedge is generally more expensive than a futures hedge, but retains some of the benefits of a favourable movement in the cash market.

Hedging with Eurodollar options

Example 10.1 The Eurodollar Options Hedge

Suppose a company treasurer, in the light of a significant drop in interest rates, becomes concerned about the possibility of higher interest rates. He takes the view that interest rates may well continue to decline but only slightly and that an increase in interest rates, although probable, will be difficult to forecast and certainly damaging to his corporation. He has a $US10,000,000 term loan rollover in three months time which will be fixed on 18 September. The three month LIBOR is now $8\frac{1}{4}\%$ and the September futures price is 91.80 (8.2% equivalent yield). The treasurer's objectives are as follows: to avoid the penalty of interest rates going up between now and his rollover date but to avoid being locked in if interest rates continue their downward trend. If his intention was to fix the price of the rollover as closely as possible to today's rates, then he would sell 10 September Eurodollar contracts at a price of 91.80. This would set his borrowing cost at 8.2%. Under certain circumstances, this might be very acceptable, as the strategy of the hedge could have been not only to fix current rates but also to have certainty as to the actual cost of funds.

However, the company treasurer may want the opportunity to take advantage of interest rates if they go down. He needs, therefore, to sell Eurodollar futures for September delivery at today's prices if prices decrease (rates rise) but to do nothing if the September price goes higher than today's price (rates continue to decline). He can achieve this by buying a put option to put (sell) September Eurodollar futures at 92.00 (Eurodollar futures option strike prices are in intervals of 50 basis points). Suppose this will cost him 37 ticks or $US925 per contract.

Best guaranteed borrowing rate

Current futures rate	+	Option premium
(8)		(0.37) = 8.37%

Hedge structure

Buy 10 September 92.00 puts
Cost = 10 × 37 × $25 = $9250

At the rollover date two outcomes are possible: the first is that three month Eurodollar rates have risen to 10.00% and his rollover is priced at that rate. The underlying futures contracts has also performed in line with this movement and the exchange delivery settlement price (EDSP) is set at 90.00 accordingly.

Profit on option
(92.00 − 90.00) × $US25 = $US5,000 per contract.

Taking into account the cost of the option of 37 ticks, the net profit is:

89

Interest rate options

$$\$5,000 - (37 \times \$25) = \$4075$$

The treasurer, therefore, has \$4,075 per \$1,000,000 of three month loan to apply against the rollover cost of 10.00%. The net borrowing rate is calculated as follows:

$$\left\{ \frac{10,000,000 \times [0.10 \times (\frac{3}{12})] - 40,750}{10,000,000} \right\} \times 4\%$$

$= 8.37\%$, exactly as guaranteed

The second possible outcome is that rates have dropped and three month Eurodollars have moved down to 6%. The rollover is set at 6% and the EDSP is set at 94.00. Obviously there is no point in exercising the option to sell at 92.00, so the treasurer allows the option to expire. In establishing the actual cost of his rollover he adds on the 37 basis points (i.e. the cost of the option) to the rollover rate of 6% to come up with a final cost of 6.37%, or:

$$\left\{ \frac{10,000,000 \times [0.06 \times (\frac{3}{12})] + 9,250}{10,000,000} \right\} \times 4$$

$= 6.37\%$

10.7 Futures Hedge

It is interesting to see what would have happened if the treasurer had simply sold ten September Eurodollar futures at 91.80. If rates have risen to 10% the EDSP is 90.00 giving a profit of $91.80 - 90.00 = 180$ ticks, and an all-in cost of funds of 8.2%.

$$\left\{ \frac{\$10,000,000 \times [0.10 \times (3/12)] - (180 \times \$25 \times 10)}{10,000,000} \right\} \times 4$$
$= 8.20\%$

This slightly outperforms the 8.37%, fixed under the options hedge. When rates fell to 6%, however, the treasurer would still have been in at 8.2% (at 6% the EDSP is 94.00, giving a 220 tick loss per contract):

$$\left\{ \frac{\$10,000,000 \times [0.06 \times (3/12)] + (220 \times \$25 \times 10)}{10,000,000} \right\} \times 4$$
$= 8.20\%$

whereas the option price fix would have been 6.37%. This example is shown graphically in Figure 10.4. It is clear that the hedger who uses options is able to hedge and simultaneously take advantage of rate movements in his favour. The straight futures hedger will always risk

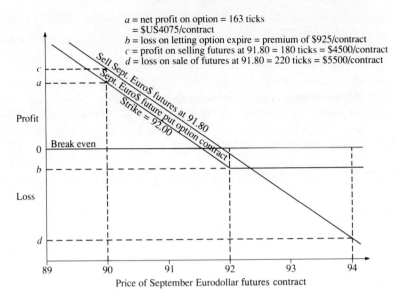

Figure 10.4 Hedging using Eurodollar options versus Eurodollar futures

making the wrong decision because, despite the conversion, he is actually taking a new position which may or may not go his way.

Nevertheless, because the option is an option on a futures contract, if one is hedging an exposure date different from a futures delivery date, an options hedge has the same level of basis risk as the equivalent futures hedge. Moreover, a downward shift in volatility will reduce option premiums for any given future price below that originally expected and introduce volatility risk to that of basis risk.

10.8 Rules for Options and Futures Hedging

The five basic rules for options and futures hedging are as follows:

1. If a future borrowing is certain to occur, hedge it by selling Eurodollar futures. If it is uncertain, hedge it by buying Eurodollar put options. This way you stand to lose only the option premium.
2. If a future lending or investment is certain, hedge it by buying Eurodollar futures. If it is uncertain, hedge it by buying Eurodollar call options.
3. Always hedge with long option positions (i.e. buy) rather than short

option positions. (The seller undertakes to hedge the volatility risk in return for the premium.)

4. Delta neutral hedges can be used if it is desired to keep the cash position insulated from interest rate risk on a continuous basis rather than at a specific point in time. This type of hedge can, however, require continuous adjustment as options deltas change.

5. Remember that option hedging is like buying insurance. The hedger must decide what level of risk he is willing to accept and what level of insurance premium he is prepared to pay.

CHAPTER 11

Forward rate agreements

11.1 Introduction

A Forward (Future) Rate Agreement (FRA) is an agreement between two parties to protect themselves against future movements in interest rates. The two parties involved agree an interest rate for a specified period of time and a specified future settlement date, based on an agreed principal amount:

- The buyer: is the party to the FRA wishing to protect itself against a future rise in the relevant interest rate.
- The seller: is the party to the FRA wishing to protect itself against a future fall in the relevant interest rate.

No commitment is made by either party to lend or borrow the principal amount. The exposure to both parties is only the interest difference between the agreed rate and the settlement price based on market rates and set by an independent body mutually accepted by both parties. The British Bankers' Association (BBA) has established a panel of twelve banks for the purpose of setting interest settlement rates. The rates are fixed by reference to deposit rates on the London interbank market at 11.00 a.m. each day. Quotations are obtained from eight banks on the panel and the middle four are averaged to give the interest settlement rate. The BBA rates differ from LIBOR in being expressed in decimals rather than fractions. As the principal amounts never exchange hands, the FRA is an off-balance sheet item and exposure is limited to the compensation payment.

11.2 Characteristics of the FRA

- *Simple agreement:* an FRA takes the form of a simple agreement between two parties who confirm details directly between themselves.
- *Flexible features:* notional principal amount, start dates and interest periods are fixed by agreement between the parties. FRAs can be tailor-made to fit customers' different requirements.

Forward rate agreements

- *Direct settlement:* there is no central clearing facility and no initial or variation margins are involved. The only funds transfer is the single compensatory payment which is made at the commencement of the interest period to which it relates.
- *Early close out:* an FRA hedge can be closed out at any stage by entering into an equal and opposite FRA at a new price. This price will reflect the market rate for the period at the time of closing the hedge.

11.3 FRA Applications

FRAs can be used to:

(a) lock in the cost of borrowing on existing floating rate loans up to two years;
(b) guarantee for up to two years the rate of interest a company will pay on future drawdowns;
(c) guarantee up to two years in advance the rate of interest on surplus funds for any period.

These facilities are widely available in US dollars, sterling, Deutschmarks and Swiss francs.

Example 11.1 FRA transaction example

Suppose that a company has a floating rate loan of $US25,000,000 with rollover occurring every six months. The treasurer is concerned about exposure to an increase in interest rates on the next rollover date in four months time and, therefore, contacts a bank to commence a hedging strategy involving FRAs. The bank quotes an FRA rate of $8\frac{1}{2}$–$8\frac{3}{8}$% for four months against ten months. This is the six month interbank market rate commencing four months ahead. The company decides to lock itself into the offered rate of $8\frac{1}{2}$% and the deal is agreed.

   In four months' time, on the settlement date, if the six months market rate has risen, say 2% (to $10\frac{1}{2}$%) the company would be entitled to gross compensation of 2% on $US25,000,000 for six months at the rate of $10\frac{1}{2}$%. The discount recognises that the FRA interest is settled at the beginning of the period and that interest is payable on that interest, whereas interest on the rollover loan is not due until the end of the period. The formulae for calculating compensation and the discounting factor are as follows:

$$\text{Compensation payment} = \frac{(M - F) \times P \times C}{360 \times 100}$$

where
M = market price
F = FRA price

94

P = notional price
C = contract period (in days)

$$\text{Discount amount} = \text{compensation payment} \times \frac{1}{1 + \left[\dfrac{(M \times C)}{360 \times 100)} \right]}$$

In the above example the outcome would be:

$$\text{Compensation payment} = \frac{(10\tfrac{1}{2} - 8\tfrac{1}{2}) \times 25,000,000 \times 181}{360 \times 100}$$

$$= \$US251,388.89$$

$$\text{Discounted amount:} = \$US251,388.89 \times \frac{1}{1 + \left[\dfrac{(10\tfrac{1}{2} \times 181}{360 \times 100)} \right]}$$

$$= \$US238,783.13$$

In this example, therefore, the bank would pay the company $US238,783.13 on the settlement date and the FRA contract between the two parties would expire. If interest rates had fallen by 2%, the company would pay the bank $US238,783.13 but as the rollover rate on their loan would have been cheaper by an equivalent percentage, the company would have still been completely hedged.

11.4 Pricing of FRAs

When calculating FRA prices both the equivalent forward–forward cash rate and the yield through the futures covering the period must be taken into account. The forward rate is the rate from the settlement date to the maturity date of the contract. This can be calculated from the spot-settlement and spot-maturity cash prices. The following example clarifies this point: suppose we needed to calculate the price of a five against eight month FRA, i.e. three month rate in five months' time, with the following dates: 15 July–17 October with 15 February as the spot date.

Cash Prices

Spot – 15 July $8\tfrac{1}{8}$, 8 (151 days)
Spot – 17 October $8\tfrac{1}{8}$, 8 (245 days)

The above set of circumstances could apply to a company that wants to borrow for three months but in five months' time. The effective interest rate could be constructed artificially by borrowing and lending simultaneously but for different maturities. This process is referred to as a forward–forward operation and in the above example would involve the company borrowing for eight months and lending for five, giving a net position of a three month loan in five months' time.

The effective interest rate is derived from the five and eight month cash rates. For instance (from the above) the eight month borrowing rate is at an annualised rate of $8\frac{1}{8}\%$ per annum, whilst the five month lending rate is 8% per annum. The forward–forward price (on offer) for the period 15 July – 18 October is calculated as follows:

$$\left\{\left[\frac{1+(0.08125 \times (245/360))}{1+(0.08 \times (151/360))}\right]-1\right\} \times \frac{360}{94}$$

$$=8.056\% \text{ per annum}$$

Futures Yield

> Futures dates   15 June and 14 September
> June futures price 91.96 September futures price 91.82
> June contract $=61$ days at 91.96 (15 July–14 September)
> Sept. contract $=33$ days at 91.82 (14 September–17 October)
> 94 days at 91.91 (weighted average)

The effective price, therefore, of guaranteeing three month interest rates in five months' time via futures is 8.09% per annum ($100-91.91$), compared with 8.056% via the forward–forward cash market. In this particular instance, the futures yield would be taken as the major indicator of the FRA price, as neither the five nor eight month periods are regular cash periods. Accordingly, a typical quotation for the period might be 8.15%–8.05%.

If the period had been, say, three against six months, six against nine months, nine against twelve months, or, six against twelve months, etc., the yield on the forward–forward cash price would have been the main indicator of price as all of these periods correspond to those in the cash market.

11.5   Arbitrage between FRAs and the Cash Markets

There will, of course, be opportunities to arbitrage between FRAs and the cash market. For instance, suppose we consider a six against twelve month period with the following cash market rates and futures prices:

Six months' cash	$8\frac{1}{16}$–8
Twelve months' cash	$8\frac{3}{16}$–$8\frac{1}{8}$
June futures contract	91.96
September futures contract	91.81
December futures contract	91.62

By using the method previously outlined, the period yields 8.32% per annum through the futures market and 8.05% per annum through the cash market (using 8% for the six month and $8\frac{3}{16}$% for the twelve month cash). The FRA would, therefore, be priced around 8.22%–8.18% for the period, making it possible to raise funds via the cash market at 8.05% and lend them at 8.18% through the FRA market. This is an effective method of arbitrage but a significant disadvantage is that the borrowing and lending on the cash markets will appear on the corporate balance sheet, potentially aggravating what may already be a tenuous situation.

11.6   Arbitrage between FRAs and Futures

Similar opportunities exist for arbitrage between FRAs and futures. For example, if we were to take June–September periods:

      Suppose   June–September yields 8.05%

                   June–September FRA is quoted as 8.05%–7.95%

If a company could obtain the FRA at the base of the market (i.e. 7.95%) and then buy the June futures contract at 9.96 (yielding 8.04%) it could lock in a small nine basis points profit. However, initial margin and the possibility of variation margin being subsequently paid, must be taken into account, particularly when working on such a small margin.

CHAPTER 12

Gilt futures

12.1 Introduction

The UK gilt-edged cash market represents a large proportion of the UK capital market with turnover increasing substantially in recent years (see Figure 12.1). The players in the market are such that they include virtually all the major financial institutions in the UK and this rapid growth in turnover has increased the need for new hedging mechanisms. Gilt futures contracts are designed to match both ends of the cash gilt market: the short gilt contract is closely associated with gilt prices of maturities between three and four-and-a-half years and the long gilt contract is associated with gilt prices of maturities between 15 and 25 years.

As redemption yields (the rate of interest at which the total discounted values of future payments of income and capital equate to the current total

Figure 12.1 Growth in UK gilt-edged market: 1980–7

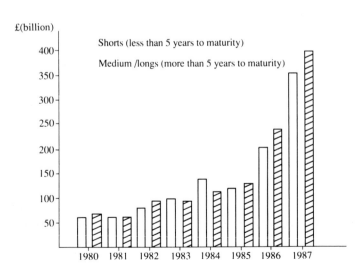

price) of gilt stocks change in line with market interest rates, gilt prices can change dramatically. Gilt futures are thus designed both as a hedge against this gilt price risk and as an efficient and liquid trading instrument.

12.2 Gilt Futures Contracts

Long-term interest rates and, therefore, gilt prices have shown substantial volatility over recent years and gilt futures provide cash gilt holders with the opportunity to hedge against longer term interest rate risk by putting on opposite positions in the gilt futures market. If gilt yields were to behave similarly at both the short and long end of the market, the long gilt contract would provide a satisfactory hedging vehicle for all types of gilt. This, however, is not the case. Just as overall rates display considerable volatility, so the shape and slope of the cash gilt yield curve can alter rapidly over time. Figure 12.2 (below) shows the cash gilt yield curve at November 1984 and approximately three months later. The significant change in the shape of the curve, as well as the sharp rise in gilt redemption yields, is apparent. Over the period in question, five year gilt yields rose by some 1.6%, while 20 year gilt yields rose by only 1%. Such behaviour has subsequently been repeated many times over.

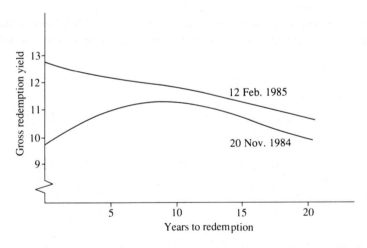

Figure 12.2 The changing shape of the cash gilt yield curve

12.3 Gilt Options Contracts

The option on the long gilt future provides an alternative hedging vehicle to maintain profit potential on the cash gilt position. Gilt futures and options together with the three month sterling interest rate futures contract, mean that hedging mechanisms are available for most types of sterling interest rate exposure and a wide range of trading activities.

Long and short gilt futures and options contracts also provide a degree of flexibility in hedging and trading, which is somewhat limited in the cash market. Although the system of physical delivery ensures that cash gilt and futures prices will remain closely in line, futures positions can be opened and closed-out extremely quickly on LIFFE at low commission costs. Gilt futures contracts also provide all market participants with the ability to 'short' the gilt market, i.e. to adopt a position anticipating a rise in yields and a fall in prices – a facility rarely available in the cash market.

A gilt futures contract provides the means for a holder of gilts to generate compensating gains from a movement in interest rates which would adversely affect the value of his cash gilt position. In this way the hedger has a degree of control over the effective selling price of a wide variety of cash gilts at a specific date or range of dates in the future. On delivery day, i.e. any business day during a delivery month, the seller of a LIFFE gilt contract is entitled to deliver at a specific price, £100,000 nominal per lot in the case of the short gilt contract or £50,000 nominal per lot in the case of the long gilt contract of any deliverable gilt.

Example 12.1 Gilt futures

A holder of £50,000 nominal of Treasury $12\frac{1}{2}$% 2003–05 sells a December long gilt futures contract at a price of $1072\frac{5}{32}$nds. This fixes a clean price (market price minus accrued interest) for delivery of this gilt in December of:

$$1072\tfrac{5}{32} \times (1.0352618)^* = 111.\tfrac{19}{32}\text{nds.}$$

*This figure is the bond price factor.

The money equivalent of this is

$$111.19 \times £500 = £55,796.88$$

NB: the unit of trading of the contract is £50,000 and the price is per £100 nominal. Therefore

$$\frac{£50,000}{100} = £500$$

This example is very simplified. As 111.19 is a 'clean price' an adjustment is made for accrued interest at settlement as explained later. In addition such a hedge would need to be ratioed (again this is explained later).

When handling prices of gilt futures and options, the user should always remember that long gilt futures are priced in 32nds (108.8 equals 108 and $\tfrac{8}{32}$nds), while short gilt futures and long gilt options are priced in 64ths (99.47 is equivalent to 99 and $\tfrac{47}{64}$ths).

12.4 Margining

Margining for gilt futures and options is carried out in the same way as for other futures contracts with positions being marked to market, using daily market prices. Initial margins for an options position will be determined relative to the estimated risk of that position and indicated by a risk factor identified daily by the Exchange.

12.5 The Delivery System

The terms of the LIFFE gilt contracts permit delivery of a range of cash stocks with different maturities and coupon rates. In the cash market, the prices of these stocks reflect the pattern and size of the income stream that each will generate to redemption. Such income differences are also reflected in the amount the buyer will be required to pay the seller (at the final settlement date) for any eligible deliverable gilt he chooses to deliver. A final list of deliverable gilts with their price factors and accrued interest is published approximately two weeks prior to the first delivery day of the delivery month.

The LIFFE delivery process involves the seller giving notice of intended delivery two business days prior to the nominated delivery day. On the delivery day, the specific gilt nominated by the seller will be delivered and the seller will receive from the buyer the relevant invoice amount. The invoicing amount is based on the Exchange Delivery Settlement Price (EDSP) as detailed in the individual contract specifications on the second business day prior to the settlement day (i.e. the day of delivery).

Short Gilt

> Invoicing amount = [EDSP × price factor × £1,000] + accrued interest

Long Gilt

> Invoicing amount = [EDSP × price factor × £500] + accrued interest

The difference lies in the unit of trading of the gilt futures contracts: long gilt future £50,000 nominal value and short gilt £100,000 nominal value.

The delivery system for a gilt option simply involves the conversion of the option into a long or short gilt futures position.

101

12.6 LIFFE Price Factors

The relationship between financial futures contracts written on such long term instruments as long term gilts in the UK or Treasury bonds in the United States and the underlying cash instruments is quite complex. It is necessary for the exchanges to determine a method of translating the price of a futures contract into an equivalent price for a cash instrument. The function of the price factor is to provide a means of bringing the various deliverable bonds with different coupons and maturities onto a common basis for delivery.

For the LIFFE long gilt contract, the definition of the price factor is the price per pound nominal value of a stock, at which the stock has a gross redemption yield of 12%. Accrued interest at 12% is included in the discounting process and the accrued interest at the actual rate is subtracted from the price factor. These price factors are calculated as of the first day of the delivery month. How to calculate these factors is shown below.

Consider first of all an ordinary yield to maturity on redemption yield calculation, ignoring accrued interest

$$P = \left[\sum_{t=1}^{n} \frac{C/2}{(1+r)^t} \right] + \frac{100}{(1+r)^n}$$

where

P = market price per £100 nominal of the bond
$C/2$ = half-yearly interest payment
n = number of half-years to redemption
r = gross redemption yield on a semi-annual basis

Ignoring accrued interest, what would the price have to be to yield 12% on an annual basis?

$$P = \left[\sum_{t=1}^{n} \frac{C/2}{[1+(0.12/2)]^t} \right] + \frac{100}{[1+(0.12/2)]^n}$$

$$= \frac{C}{2(0.06)} \left[1 - \frac{1}{(1.06)^n} \right] + \frac{100}{(1.06)^n}$$

$$= \frac{C}{0.12} \left[1 - \frac{1}{(1.06)^n} \right] + \frac{100}{(1.06)^n}$$

Adjustments have to be made for accrued interest because the first day of the delivery month does not coincide with interest payments on the gilt. This is done by adding the price shown above, which determines the price at an interest payment date, to the next coupon payment and discounting the whole sum back to the present at an annual rate of 12%. To get a clean price, subtract the amount of accrued interest on the stock between the

102

previous interest payment date and the settlement date on the first day of the delivery month.

$$P = \frac{1}{1.06^x/182.5} \left\{ C^* + \frac{C}{0.12} \left[1 - \frac{1}{(1.06)^n} \right] + \frac{100}{(1.06)^n} \right\} - \frac{C}{2} \left[\frac{y-x}{182.5} \right]$$

For the short gilt contract the clean price is calculated so the deliverable stock has a gross redemption yield of 10% per annum. The formula is then:

$$P = \frac{1}{1.05^x/182.5} \left[C^* + \frac{C}{0.1} \left(1 - \frac{1}{1.05} \right) + \frac{100}{1.05} \right] - \frac{C}{2} \left[\frac{y-x}{182.5} \right]$$

where

$C/2 =$ half-yearly interest payments
$P =$ clean price of the gilt
$n =$ no. of half-years to redemption from next interest payment date
$C^* =$ next interest payment which will usually be $C/2$ but is zero if the stock is ex-divided
$x =$ number of days from and including the first day of the delivery month, up to but excluding the next payment day.
$y =$ no. of days after the previous interest payment date, up to and including the next payment date.

If the stock is ex-dividend (i.e. without dividend) on the first day of the delivery month, the final term in the equation above will be $+ C/2[(y-x)/182.5]$ rather than negative. The price factor or conversion factor is then calculated in accordance with the following simple formula:

Price factor $\dfrac{P}{100}$

Such conversion factors determine the invoice price for a gilt ex-delivery. For instance, suppose you decide to deliver Treasury $11\frac{3}{4}\%$ 2003–2007 stock against a December futures contract with interest payment dates 22 January and 22 July. On 1 March the price factor calculated from the above formula is 0.9819012. There are 131 days between the last payment date of 22 July and 1 December, hence with a daily accrued interest of

$$\frac{£(0.1175 \times 50,000)}{365} = £16.0959$$

there is accrued interest of £2,108.56 attached to the stock. If the settlement price on the gilt was 102.15, the settlement value on delivery of Treasury $11\frac{3}{4}\%$ 2003–2007 would be

$$S = (102.15 \times 0.9819 \times £500) + 2,108.56$$
$$= £52,415.70 \text{ for } £50,000 \text{ nominal delivered}$$

Gilt futures

Table 12.1. Profits from delivery of gilts

Stock	Futures price	Price factor	Implied price	Clean* price	Profit from delivery
$11\frac{3}{4}\%$ 2003–2007	114.07	0.9819012	112.05	112.28	$+\frac{41}{32}$
$12\frac{1}{2}\%$ 2003–2005	114.07	0.9753008	111.13	113.17	$-\frac{68}{32}$
8% 2002–2006	114.07	0.6942727	79.10	80.07	$-\frac{29}{32}$

*Market price less accrued interest.

The procedure for US Treasury bond contracts is similar to that for gilts and is discussed in a later section.

12.7 Cheapest to Deliver Gilts

What do these conversion or price factors imply? First the invoice prices of gilts are not dependent upon the actual price of gilts in the cash market. The conversion factors assume a completely flat yield curve at 12% and 10% for long term and short term gilts respectively: this may not be the case in the cash market where at various times one observes both upward sloping and downward sloping yield curves.

Differences between cash yields and futures yields could arise from tax considerations, liquidity premiums, risk premiums or market segmentation. If there are differences between cash market prices adjusted by the relevant price factor and the futures price, it is evident that some particular gilts (or T-bonds) will be cheaper to deliver than others. The choice of the actual gilt stock to be delivered lies with the seller of the futures contract. In order to assess a fair price for the contract the buyer must anticipate receiving that gilt which will create the maximum profit or minimum loss for the seller who makes delivery. Consider the following set of price information given in Table 12.1. Looking at these prices, the Treasury $11\frac{3}{4}\%$ 2003–2007 is the cheapest to delivery (CTD) compared with the other gilts. Since buying in the market and delivering into the futures market creates a cash gain rather than a cash loss. In general, the cheapest deliverable instrument tends to be the highest coupon gilt and/or the one most recently issued. Because one financial instrument is usually the optimal instrument to deliver, the futures markets in gilts (and T-bonds) tend to be priced off the cheapest deliverable instruments, i.e. prices in the futures market will generally move in line with prices of the cheapest deliverable instrument adjusted for the price factor.

12.8 Cash and Carry Arbitrage

This phrase is used to describe a combined futures and cash market arbitrage strategy whereby an investor runs a matched position, holding gilts and at the same time being short of an equal nominal amount of futures. Although involving a long gilt edged stock and a long dated futures, this is a short term money operation, the overall return being the balance of profits/losses on the two offsetting positions taken between instigation and the chosen delivery date.

September
Buy gilt
Sell December   Delivery   December
    Long gilt contract   Hold*   Month start   Month end

*Incur financing cost of gilt position
Accrue gilt coupon

The decision whether to deliver against a futures contract at the beginning or end of a delivery month will basically depend upon the relationship between the running yield on the gilt and the financing cost of the position. If a trader earns more on the gilt position in accrued interest then he pays in financing cost, then it makes sense to maintain the position as long as possible by delivering at the end of the delivery month. If the reverse is true, then it makes sense to deliver as early as possible at the beginning of the month. The deliverable gilt which shows the largest 'cash and carry' profit/smallest loss will be the cheapest to deliver instrument. This strategy is of limited use when trading gilts as it is normally found that only one or two gilt edged stocks are priced cheaply enough relative to futures to produce high enough return to make these strategies attractive. This is because of the uneven yield in the gilt edged market.

12.9 Basis Risk

The close relationship between the gilt futures price and the cheapest to deliver gilt means that the gilt future should provide an excellent hedging mechanism for a holding of the cheapest to deliver gilt. In fact such a hedge for a likely delivery day should be nearly perfect because of the basis convergence that has taken place up to that day. Basis in respect of gilt futures contracts is defined as the 'futures price equivalent' of the cheapest to deliver gilt minus the actual futures price.

$$\text{Basis} = \frac{\text{Clean price of cheapest to deliver gilt}}{\text{price factor}} - \text{futures price}$$

105

Gilt futures

Since the gilt delivery process at LIFFE takes only three business days, and on the assumption that arbitrage profits immediately prior to delivery are likely to be small, this basis should be almost eliminated on the probable delivery day. If, however, a hedge of the cheapest to deliver gilt is unwound prior to the delivery month, changes in the short term financing costs could affect the basis, changing it from its expected value at the time the hedge was instituted.

Example 12.2 Basis change
Long gilt December delivery 11 September
Cheapest to deliver stock Treasury $11\frac{3}{4}\%$ 2003–2007
Clean price 112.28
Price factor 0.9819012
Futures price 114.07

Basis = (112.28/0.9819012) − 114.07 = 0.7368

0.7368

Expected basis = 0.35

| 8 Sept. | 44 days | 22 Oct. | 40 days | 1 Dec. |

Figure 12.3   Expected basis on gilts

In Figure 12.3 it is assumed that delivery will take place on 1 December because short term rates are currently higher than the running yield of the cash gilt. If the cost of financing or the cheapest to deliver gilt price changes, then the basis on 22 October may well turn out to be different to the expected interpolation of 0.35. The hedger will have reduced his original interest rate exposure to this smaller basis risk. Hedging gilts other than the cheapest to deliver stocks against the short and long gilt futures will need more careful design, because two basis risks will be involved: the basis risk between the cheapest to deliver gilt price and the futures price and the basis risk between the cheapest to deliver price and the price of the gilt being hedged.

For a non-CTD gilt

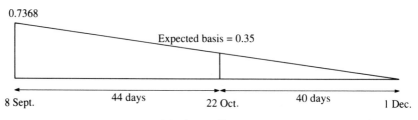

$$\text{Overall basis} = \underbrace{\left[\frac{\text{Price of gilt}}{\text{Price factor}}\right] - \left[\frac{\text{Price of CTD}}{\text{CTD price factor}}\right]}_{A}$$

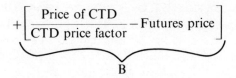

$$+ \underbrace{\left[\frac{\text{Price of CTD}}{\text{CTD price factor}} - \text{Futures price} \right]}_{B}$$

Part A of the formula will obviously be zero for the cheapest to deliver gilt. Although part B is a function of the cost of carry (difference between futures and cash rates) and is expected to decline steadily to near zero at delivery, part A is much harder to predict and will depend on the shape of the yield curve, tax effects, etc.

12.10   Hedging with Gilt Futures Contracts

Hedging with gilt futures falls naturally into the three following categories:

(a)   hedging a cash position in the cheapest to deliver gilt;
(b)   hedging cash holdings of other gilt edged stocks;
(c)   hedging sterling-denominated bonds other than gilts, such as sterling corporate bonds, local authority bonds, etc.

The essence of achieving a good gilt futures hedge involves choosing hedge ratios that equate the price volatility of the bond being hedged to that of the cheapest deliverable gilt, which in turn is linked to price movements of the gilt futures contract by its price factor.

12.11   Hedging the Cheapest to Deliver Gilt

Because cash/futures arbitrage will lead to the price of the gilt futures being closely linked to the price of the cheapest to deliver gilt, the hedge of the CTD gilt is constructed using the price factor as the hedge ratio.

$$\frac{\text{Number of}}{\text{contracts}} = \frac{\text{Nominal value of gilt position}}{\text{Nominal value of contract}} \times \text{Price factor}$$

Example 12.3 Hedging the CTD Gilt

Assume the Treasury $12\frac{3}{4}\%$ 1992 is the cheapest to deliver gilt for the December 1987 short gilt contract. In order to hedge £3,000,000 of this gilt the holder requires:

$$\text{Number of contracts} = \frac{£3,000,000}{£100,000} \times 1.0938166 \text{ (author's estimation)}$$

= 32.8 or 33 contracts

The locked in gilt price
Date: 10 September

Gilt futures

December short gilt futures $114\frac{7}{64}$ths

Treasury 12% 1992 clean price $124\frac{58}{64}$ths

Locked in clean price 1 December (assumed day for delivery) is as follows:

Futures prices × price factor = 114.07 × 1.0938166 = $124\frac{52}{64}$

Locked in clean price for 15 November

The locked in price for a non-delivery date such as 15 November would be calculated using the period from the initiation of the hedge to the end of the delivery month:

10 September–15 November = 66 days

16 November–31 December = 46 days

Price = [124.52 × (66/112)] + [124.58 × (46/112)]

     = 73.55022 + 51.30078

     = 124.851 or $124\frac{55}{64}$

NB: as already mentioned, a hedge for a non-delivery date is inherently more risky than for a delivery date such as 1 December, because changes in financing costs and/or cash prices could alter the cash/futures relationship between 10 September and 15 November.

12.12 Hedging Other Gilts

When hedging gilts other than the cheapest to deliver, allowance must be made for the relative volatility of the cash instruments. Prices of longer maturity, low coupon gilts are more volatile than prices of shorter maturity, high coupon gilts because of sensitivity to yield changes.

$$\text{No. of contracts for gilt hedge}$$
$$= \frac{\text{Nominal value of cash gilt}}{\text{Nominal value of gilt future}}$$
$$\times \text{Relative volatility of cash gilt}$$
$$\text{and CTD gilt} \times \text{Price factor of CTD gilt}$$

There are four basic approaches to the measurement of relative volatility. The first two being (i) LIFFE price factors and (ii) regression analysis, both of which were covered in Section 8.6. However, both these methods assume that a change in interest rates will affect bonds with different coupons and maturities as dictated by the price factors. This is not the case, as relative gilt (and T-bond) volatilities are not independent of the level of interest rates. To handle this problem perturbation analysis or duration analysis can be adopted.

Perturbation analysis

Perturbation analysis examines the changes in the price of the cash instrument to be hedged and the cheapest to deliver instrument for a 1% yield change and uses the ratio to design the hedge, this is seen in Example 12.4.

Duration analysis

For reasonable changes in interest rates, the relative duration of bonds can provide yet another type of hedge ratio. To do this the duration of the gilt to be hedged is calculated along with that of the CTD instrument. This is a measure of the gilts' price responsiveness to changes in yield. The ratio of these two figures is used to design the hedge. The duration measures the impact on price of a minimal change in yield and hence contains no implicit forecast of how large the change will be over the period.

The duration based volatility is:

$$\left[\frac{1 + \text{Cheapest to deliver redemption yield}}{1 + \text{Hedge gilt redemption yield}} \right]$$

$$\times \left[\frac{\text{Clean price of gilt to be hedged}}{\text{Clean price of cheapest to deliver}} \right]$$

$$\times \left[\frac{\text{Duration of gilt to be hedged}}{\text{Duration of cheapest to deliver}} \right]$$

Each of these methods has its advantages and disadvantages. It is up to the individual user of the gilt futures contract to determine which is the most suitable for his hedging activities. The following example uses perturbation analysis:

Example 12.4 Hedging a non CTD gilt

Assume it is September 1987

	Price	Yield
Gilt held £5,000,000 Treasury $11\frac{1}{2}$% 1989	101.22	10.21
Cheapest to deliver gilt Treasury $12\frac{3}{4}$% 1992	108.14	10.21

Price factor of cheapest to deliver gilt for December contract = 1.0938166
Let us assume that the £ value of a 1% yield change per £100 nominal is as follows:

Treasury $11\frac{1}{2}$% £2.40
Treasury $12\frac{3}{4}$% £3.50

NB: these figures are for illustration only.

No. of short gilt contracts for hedge

$$= \frac{£5,000,000}{£100,000} \times \frac{2.40}{3.50} \times 1.0938166$$

$$= 37.5 \text{ or } 38 \text{ contracts}$$

Gilt futures

As noted earlier in Section 12.9, hedging gilts other than the cheapest to deliver gilt is likely to be less precise, especially if it is expected that the hedge will be lifted at a point prior to the delivery month. Even among the deliverable gilts for a specific futures contract, the relationship between the cheapest to deliver gilt and other gilts can alter substantially through time. The relative volatility measures outlined above all assume a predetermined relative yield change for the gilt to be hedged and the cheapest to deliver gilt. Depending on the actual relative yield change, the hedge result may not provide total risk reduction.

12.13 Hedging with Long Gilt Options

The number of contracts for a full gilt hedge is worked out in exactly the same way as for a full futures hedge, as each option is the right to buy or sell one gilt futures contract.

The basic strategy is that if your cash gilt position will be adversely affected by higher gilt prices (say, a delayed gilt purchase), buy gilt call options or sell gilt put options. If your cash position will be adversely affected by lower gilt prices (a cash gilt portfolio) buy gilt put options or sell call options. The best guaranteed futures price with an options hedge is always worse than the price locked in with a futures hedge, but there is always a breakdown level at which the futures price (and thus the cash gilt price) is more favourable than that which would be achieved with a straight

Figure 12.4 Alternative hedge strategies with long gilt options

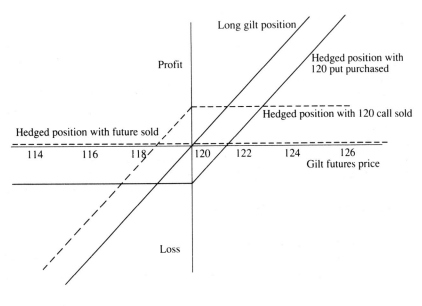

futures hedge. The alternative hedges can be seen in Figure 12.4 where it is assumed a quantity of the cheapest to deliver stock is being hedged.

Assuming basis risk is small, the futures hedge is effectively the same as liquidating the long gilt position (i.e. locking into a fixed price). The put option purchased plus the long gilt produces a net position that behaves like an artificial long call option with limited losses if the futures price ends up below 120 and potentially unlimited profits if the futures price rises. The call option sold plus the long gilt creates a net position that behaves like an artificial short put option. This reduces potential losses to the potential gains from rising gilt prices.

There are, of course, two types of option hedges: fixed hedges and delta hedges. In a fixed hedge, the exposure is hedged one to one with options. A delta hedge is designed to maintain a combined cash and options position with a zero delta. Such a hedge may need frequent rebalancing and will be more risky than a fixed hedge because the number of options required will be large. For a gilt options hedge, the correct number of contracts for a delta (or ratio hedge) involves determining the best futures hedge and then dividing by the delta of the option being used.

For a hedge of the CTD stock:

Number of options for delta hedge

$$= \frac{\text{Nominal value of gilt}}{\pounds 50,000} \times \frac{\text{Price factor}}{\text{Delta}}$$

12.14 Bond Portfolio Hedging

For portfolio managers, gilt futures and options provide a highly liquid mechanism for protecting all or part of a portfolio from rising interest rates without selling the cash gilts (which could involve high commissions and may move the market in the particular stock against the seller). It enables the active portfolio manager to lower and raise the potential volatility of a gilt portfolio at will. The manager can make his gilt portfolio less sensitive to interest rate movements when he expects rates to rise and more sensitive when he expects rates to fall. Gilt futures and options can also help improve gilt switching effectiveness by making it easier to offset any impact of a switch on portfolio volatility. Finally, by locking in sales prices for cash gilts, gilt futures can allow portfolio managers to transfer profits from one accounting period to another, thus improving both profit and tax planning. A typical example of a portfolio hedge follows.

Example 12.5 Portfolio hedging

Suppose a bank portfolio manager has a small portfolio of long-dated gilts and is worried that rising interest rates over the next couple of

Gilt futures

months will depress gilt prices. On the assumption that the current date is 3 September, he decides to look at the possibility of hedging the 'clean' value (i.e. market value less accrued interest) of his portfolio with gilt futures.

Stock	Nominal value	Clean* price	Redemption yield*	Market value	Duration*	Price factor
Treasury 13½% 2004–2008	£20m	$124\frac{17}{32}$	10.1	£24,906,250	7.67	1.1053256
Treasury 12½% 2003–2005	£10m	$115\frac{13}{32}$	10.1	£11,540,625	7.62	1.0345306
Treasury 8% 2009	£10m	$82\frac{10}{32}$	9.7	£8,231,250	8.96	0.6942022

December long gilt futures price = 114.25

*These figures are adopted purely for illustrative purposes.

1. Determine the number of contracts for a full hedge

Treasury 13½% 2004–2008 (cheapest to deliver)

$$= \frac{£20,000,000}{£50,000} \times 1.1053256$$

= 442 contracts

Treasury 12½% 2003–2005   Relative volatility

$$= \frac{1.1010}{1.1010} \times \frac{115.13}{124.17} \times \frac{7.62}{7.67}$$

= 0.92

No. of contracts

$$= \frac{£10,000,000}{£50,000} \times 0.92 \times 1.1053256$$

= 190 contracts

Treasury 8% 2009   Relative volatility

$$= \frac{1.1010}{1.0970} \times \frac{82.10}{124.17} \times \frac{8.96}{7.67}$$

= 0.78

No. of contracts

$$= \frac{£10,000,000}{£50,000} \times 0.78 \times 1.1053256$$

= 172 contracts

Total hedge = 804 contracts

Sell 804 September long gilt futures at 114.25

2. Determine expected value of Portfolio on 31 October (2 months on)
Assume delivery day of 1 December on which the expected price of the CTD gilt is 125.00.

112

Bond portfolio hedging

3 September–31 October = 58 days

31 October–1 December = 31 days

Expected clean price of cheapest to deliver = $(124.17 \times \frac{31}{89}) + (125.00 \times \frac{58}{89})$

$$= 124.84$$

This represents a price change of 0.3088 in the cheapest to deliver. This will be accompanied by expected price changes in the other two stocks, determined by their price volatility relative to the CTD.

Expected price change for Treasury $12\frac{1}{2}$% 2003–2005

$= 0.3088 \times 0.92$

$= 0.2841$

Expected price change for Treasury 8% 2009

$= 0.3088 \times 0.78$

$= 0.2049$

Therefore:

	Expected clean price	Market value (£)
Treasury $13\frac{1}{2}$% 2004–2008	124.84	24,968,000
Treasury $12\frac{1}{2}$% 2003–2005	115.69	11,569,000
Treasury 8% 2009	82.52	8,552,000

Expected portfolio value = £45,089,000

Portfolio hedge result 31 October

September long gilt futures price = 116.05

	Nominal value	Clean price	Redemption yield	Market value (£)
Treasury $13\frac{1}{2}$% 2004–2008	£20m	126.30	9.9	25,387,500
Treasury $12\frac{1}{2}$% 2003–2005	£10m	117.16	9.9	11,750,000
Treasury 8% 2009	£10m	85.13	10.5	8,540,625

Total £45,678,125

Futures loss = $804 \times £15.525$ (tick size) $\times 44 = -£552,750$

Hence the effective value of the portfolio is (45,678,125 − 552,750) = £45,125,375. This is close to the expected value of £45,089,000; consequently, the long gilt hedge has been effective. Note that the hedge is not regarded as ineffective because the futures position lost money. The effectiveness of the hedge is measured by the success with which the expected portfolio value is achieved. In this case the redemption yields in the different gilts moved closely in line. If this were not the case then an

Gilt futures

excellent hedge would be achieved if the overall portfolio redemption yield moved in line with the yield on the cheapest to deliver. This is likely for a well diversified portfolio assuming the CTD is a representative long gilt.

The alternative of an options hedge can also be considered
Let us assume that a current set of prices for the December long gilt options looks like the following:

Exercise price	Put (%)	Delta	Call (%)	Delta
112	1.58	(− 0.35)	4.44	(0.65)
114	2.48	(− 0.45)	3.34	(0.55)
116	3.51	(− 0.55)	2.37	(0.45)

Four alternative options hedges are shown below
(a)   fixed hedge with calls: sell 804 114.00 calls at 3.34
(b)   ratio hedge with calls: sell 804/0.55 or 1462 114.00 calls
(c)   fixed hedge with puts: buy 804 114.00 puts at 2.48
(d)   ratio hedge with puts: sell 804/0.45 or 1787 114.00 puts

Assuming on 31 October that the volatility is the same, the prices may be:

Exercise price	Put (%)	Delta	Call (%)	Delta
112	0.61	− 0.24	5.25	0.76
114	1.37	− 1.34	4.01	0.66
116	2.27	− 0.46	2.55	0.54

The alternative hedges thus show the following results:

(a)   3.34 − 4.01 =   = 0.33
   = 33 × 804 × £7.8125 (tick size)
   = − £207,281.25

(b)   3.34 − 4.01   = 0.33
   = 33 × 1,462 × £7.8125
   = − £376,921.87

(c)   2.48 − 1.37   = 1.11 (= 75/64)
   = 75 × 804 × £7.8125
   = − £471,093.75

(d)   2.48 − 1.37   = 1.11
   = 75 × 1,787 × £7.8125
   = − £1,047,070.31

These results give effective portfolio values as follows:

Hedge	Profit/loss (£)	Effective portfolio value (£)
Futures	− 552,750	45,125,375
(a) Fixed option hedge (calls)	− 207,613	45,470,512

(b)	Ratio hedge	− 376,922	45,301,203
(c)	Fixed option hedge (puts)	− 471,094	45,207,031
(d)	Ratio hedge	− 1,047,070	44,631,055

As can be seen a wide variety of different terminal portfolio values is achieved. As the cash position moved in favour of the hedger, the fixed option hedges did better than the futures hedge and because the cash price movements were modest the call hedge outperforms the put hedge.

12.15 Conclusion

From this chapter it can be seen that gilt contracts provide an efficient means of hedging many exposures. Portfolio managers can lock in future buying or selling prices for a whole range of gilt maturities. The contracts can also be used to hedge a variety of sterling denominated bonds other than gilts. With the continued development of the primary dealer market (along with an increase in the size of risk books being operated) and a substantial rise in gilt turnover, the requirement for hedging quickly and easily through gilt futures and options has increased significantly. The cash efficiency of hedging on margin further emphasises the attractiveness of futures and options instruments.

CHAPTER 13

United States Treasury bond futures and options

13.1 Introduction

The US Treasury Bond (T-bond) and note market represents the largest fixed interest security market worldwide. The volume of US Treasury debt in both private and public hands has grown rapidly in the last few years in line with the expansion of the US budget deficit. This has resulted in a huge expansion of Treasury bond, note futures and options trading both in the United States and overseas. The extent of non-US holdings of US Treasury securities also emphasises the need to have such markets in non-US time zones, a fact confirmed by the activity in LIFFE T-bond futures.

As with gilt futures, T-bond futures give the hedger a degree of control over the effective selling price of a variety of cash bonds for a range of dates in the future. On delivery day the seller of a LIFFE T-bond future is allowed to deliver, at a specific price, $100,000 nominal value per contract of any deliverable Treasury bond. (Delivery can be made of any Treasury bond maturing at least fifteen years from the first day of the delivery month, if not callable. If callable the earliest call date must be at least fifteen years from the first day of the delivery month. For example, suppose a holder of $100,000 nominal of a 12% 2005–2010 Treasury bond, sells a September 1988 T-bond futures contract at a price of $81\frac{21}{32}$nds. This fixes a clean price for delivery of this bond in September of:

$$81.21 \times 1.431^* = 116.850$$

In dollar terms this would be

$$(116.85 \times \$1,000) = \$116,850$$

*The figure of 1.431 is the bond price factor.
Also the clean price is multiplied by $1,000 as the quotation basis for the T-bond future is per $100 per value, so

$$\frac{100,000}{100} = \$1,000$$

As a result the holder of the $12\frac{3}{4}\%$ 2005–2010 T-bond will receive \$131.160 for \$100,000 nominal value of stock delivered in September.

It is worth stressing that like gilts, the pricing convention for cash T-bonds and T-bond futures is in 32nds (82.09 equals $82\frac{9}{32}$nds) and options on LIFFE T-bond futures are priced in 64ths (3.42 equals $3\frac{42}{64}$ths).

13.2 Pricing of T-bond Contracts

The method of translating the price of a T-bond future into an equivalent price for the cash instrument is, like gilts, done through the price factor. The actual calculation of the price factor is similar to that for gilts but it has been simplified so that new price factors do not need to be calculated for each new delivery month. This is attained by invoicing with maturity defined only in complete quarters. For example, a 7% Treasury bond with twenty-five years seven months and ten days to go to maturity would be deemed to have a maturity of twenty-five years and six months. Odd periods are always rounded down to the nearest quarter. The exchange then simply calculates what the price of this twenty-five year six month bond will be to give an effective yield of 8%. There is no calculation of accrued interest on the bond. Consequently, although not as accurate as the gilt calculation, the T-bond price system is easier to calculate.

Given the bond described above, the price factor would be calculated as follows:

$$P = \frac{7/2}{0.04}\left[1 - \frac{1}{(1.04)^{51}}\right] + \frac{100}{(1.05)^{51}}$$
$$= 89.19$$
$$\text{Factor} = 0.8919$$

As with gilt futures, T-bond futures are priced off the cheapest to deliver bond. This is the bond with the smallest loss/greatest profit given the difference between the clean price of the cash bond and the futures implied price.

13.3 Hedging with T-bond Contracts

As with gilt futures, hedging with T-bond futures falls naturally into the three following categories:

(a) hedging a cash position in the cheapest to deliver bond;
(b) hedging cash positions of other Treasury bonds;
(c) hedging dollar denominated bonds other than Treasury bonds such as Eurobonds, or corporate bonds, etc.

United States Treasury bond

As far as (a) and (b) are concerned the produce for the hedge is very similar to that described in the preceding chapter. However, part (c) is quite an interesting situation and warrants further examination.

13.4 Hedging Dollar Bonds other than T-bonds

Although the methods for estimating relative volatility can be applied to hedges of dollar denominated bonds other than T-bonds, such hedges will probably be relatively less efficient for the two following reasons:

1. Relationships between yield changes on non-Treasury bonds and T-bonds are likely to be less stable than between different T-bonds.
2. Changes in the credit rating of non-Treasury bonds can alter the yield relationships upon which hedges are based and, therefore, decrease hedge effectiveness.

An imperfect hedge, however, is likely to do better than no hedge at all, particularly, if interest rates are especially volatile. Example 13.1 examines the effectiveness of LIFFE contracts in hedging both US Treasury bonds and Eurobonds.

Example 13.1 Hedging dollar denominated bonds

Suppose a portfolio manager has a small portfolio of dollar bonds and after a recent run-up in bond prices is concerned that a market reaction is imminent. Assuming that the current date is 18 April 1986, he therefore decides to explore the possibilities of hedging with LIFFE T-bond futures.

	Nominal value	Clean price	Redemption yield	Market value ($)
Treasury 12$\frac{3}{4}$% 2005–2010	$10m	153.11	7.50	15,334,375
Treasury 8$\frac{3}{4}$% 2003–2008	$20m	113.13	7.36	22,681,250
Eurobond A 11$\frac{5}{8}$% 1994	$5m	122$\frac{1}{2}$	7.66	6,125,000
Eurobond B 10$\frac{1}{4}$% 2000	$10m	109	9.08	10,900,000
			Total	$55,040,625

June bond futures price = 103.28
CTD (12$\frac{3}{4}$% 2005–2010) conversion factor = 1.4570

1. *Determine impact of a 0.5% change in yield on price*

	New yield	New price	Price change
Treasury 12$\frac{3}{4}$% 2005–2010	8.00	145.04	8.07
Treasury 8$\frac{3}{4}$% 2003–2008	7.86	107.20	5.25
Eurobond A 11$\frac{5}{8}$% 1994	8.16	116.16	6.00
Eurobond B 10$\frac{1}{4}$% 2000	9.58	103.02	5.30

Hedging dollar bonds other than T-bonds

2. *Determine number of contracts for full hedge*

$$\text{Treasury } 12\tfrac{3}{4}\% \; 2005-2010 \; (\text{CTD}) = \frac{\$10,000,000}{\$100,000} \times 1.4570 = 145.70$$

$$\text{Treasury } 8\tfrac{3}{4}\% \; 2003-2008 \quad = \frac{\$20,000,000}{\$100,000} \times \frac{5.25}{8.07} \times 1.4570 = 182.82$$

$$\text{Eurobond A } 11\tfrac{5}{8}\% \; 1994 \quad = \frac{\$5,000,000}{\$100,000} \times \frac{6.00}{8.07} \times 1.4570 = 53.19$$

$$\text{Eurobond B } 10\tfrac{1}{4}\% \; 2000 \quad = \frac{\$10,000,000}{\$100,000} \times \frac{5.30}{8.07} \times 1.4570 = 105.26$$

Total = 487 contracts

Sell 487 June Bond Futures at 103.28.

3. *Determine expected value of portfolio on 21 May (1 month later)*
Assume delivery day is 30 June, on which the expected price of the CTD is:

$103.28 \times 1.4570 = 151.35$

18 April–21 May = 33 days

22 May–30 June = 39 days

21 May expected clean price of cheapest to deliver

$= 153.11 \times \tfrac{39}{72} + 151.35 \times \tfrac{33}{72}$

$= 152.43$

This represents a price change of 0.91375 in the CTD. This in turn implies expected price changes in the other stocks determined by their price volatility relative to the CTD.

$$\text{Treasury } 8\tfrac{3}{4}\% \; 2003-2008 = 0.91375 \times \left(\frac{5.25}{8.07}\right) = 0.6428$$

$$\text{Eurobond A } 11\tfrac{5}{8}\% \; 1994 = 0.91375 \times \left(\frac{6.00}{8.07}\right) = 0.6671$$

$$\text{Eurobond B } 10\tfrac{1}{4}\% \; 2000 = 0.91375 \times \left(\frac{5.30}{8.07}\right) = 0.6601$$

Therefore

	Expected clean price	Market value ($)
Treasury $12\tfrac{3}{4}\%$ 2005–2010	152.43	15,243,000
Treasury $8\tfrac{3}{4}\%$ 2003–2008	112.76	22,552,000
Eurobond A $11\tfrac{5}{8}\%$ 1994	121.83	6,091,500
Eurobond B $10\tfrac{1}{4}\%$ 2000	108.34	10,834,000
Expected portfolio value		$54,720,500

Portfolio hedge result 21 May 1986
June T-bond futures price = 95.29

119

United States Treasury bond

	Clean price	Redemption yield	Yield change	Market value ($)
Treasury 12$\frac{3}{4}$% 2005–2010	140.22	8.45	+ 0.95	14,068,750
Treasury 8$\frac{3}{4}$% 2003–2008	103.30	8.32	+ 0.96	20,787,500
Eurobond A 11$\frac{5}{8}$% 1994	121.00	7.86	+ 0.20	6,050,000
Eurobond B 10$\frac{1}{4}$% 2000	105.20	9.50	+ 0.42	10,562,500
		Total portfolio value =		$51,468,750

Futures gain = 487 × $31.25 (tick size) × 255
$$= \$3,880,781.30$$
Effective value of portfolio 21 May = $55,349,531.30.

This is approximately $629,000 above the expected value of $54,720,500. While this windfall gain is good news for the hedger, it indicates a degree of hedge inefficiency because, clearly, an unexpected gain could just as easily have been an unexpected loss.

Why has the gain arisen?
The gain has arisen partly because the yield changes on the two Eurobonds in the portfolio were not as large as those on the Treasury bonds. As the futures price reflects movement in the yield on the cheapest to deliver, this created the wind-fall.

Suppose just the hedge of the Treasury bonds is considered:

Expected value = $37,795,000
Final value   = $34,856,250

Futures profit on 329 contracts = 329 × $31.25 × 255 ticks
$$= \$2,621,718.80$$
Effective value 21 May   = $37,477,969

So, even the hedge of the Treasury bond is not perfect. The reason is a change in the basis:

Expected basis 21 May $\left(\dfrac{153.11}{1.4570} - 103.28 \right) \times \dfrac{39}{72} = 1.371$

Actual basis 21 May $\left(\dfrac{140.22}{1.4570} - 95.29 \right) = 0.654$

This represents an adverse unexpected basis change of 0.717 or approximately 23 ticks.

Dollar value effect = 23 × $31.25 × 329 contracts
$$= \$236,468.75$$

This explains a large part of the unexpected $317,031 shortfall on the T-bond hedge. The remainder is due to the inaccuracy of the relative volatility calculation.

$$\text{Estimated relative volatility} = \frac{5.25}{8.07} = 0.703$$

$$\text{Actual relative volatility} = \frac{9.17}{12.21} = 0.753$$

The conclusions to be drawn from this example are threefold, as follows:

1. Though Treasury bond futures will protect the value of Eurobond portfolios against major shift in yields, there is always the possibility that Eurobond yields will not move precisely in line with T-bond yields.
2. Sharp changes in basis can occur over short periods of time, impacting on hedge efficiency.
3. It may be necessary to adjust the number of contracts to offset adverse changes in relative volatility for large yield movements.

Nevertheless, Treasury bond futures provide an efficient means of hedging major interest rate changes.

13.5 Hedging with T-bond options

The portfolio manager in our example could, as an alternative to hedging with T-bond futures, hedge with T-bond options. For example, suppose the following are T-bond June option prices for 18 April 1986:

Exercise price	Put (ticks)	Call (ticks)
102	1.04	2.63
104	1.58	1.51

Four alternative hedges are shown below:

1. Buy 487 102.00 puts at 1.04.
2. Buy 487 104.00 puts at 1.58.
3. Sell 487 102.00 calls at 2.63.
4. Sell 487 104.00 calls at 1.51.

The option prices on 21 May were:

Exercise price	Put (ticks)	Call (ticks)
102	7.44	1.00
104	9.20	0.50

United States Treasury bond

The results of the various hedges can now be calculated:

Hedge	Options position profit/loss	Effective portfolio value
(a)	+$3,226,375	$54,695,125
(b)	+$3,606,844	$55,075,594
(c)	+$966,391	$52,435,141
(d)	+$494,610	$51,963,359

Clearly, all the option hedges did significantly worse than the equivalent futures. We would expect this if prices moved against the hedge, as they did in this instance. One of the main conclusions must be the limited nature of protection offered by option hedges when the price movements of the underlying assets are large. Conversely, if yields had fallen rather than risen on the underlying bonds, the put options would have offered potentially adequate cover.

All hedge strategies carry a degree of risk. The option is an option on a futures contract; therefore the basis risk is the same as the equivalent futures hedge. With options, however, there is also the volatility risk: if volatility changes unpredictably or abruptly, then the level of option premiums for a given futures price will also change. Consequently, the options hedge requires careful selection.

13.6   Conclusion

T-bond futures, and gilt futures can provide an efficient means of hedging many exposures. They provide a highly cash efficient mechanism for trading any specific view about bond prices and/or price volatility. In addition, to the general merits of T-bond futures and options as trading and hedging vehicles, LIFFE T-bond contracts have the following major advantages compared with those traded on other exchanges:

1.   The LIFFE margining system provides the most cash efficient way of trading T-bond futures and options currently available worldwide.
2.   LIFFE imposes no limits on the price movements of Treasury bond futures and options so that a position can be offset at any time. There is no danger of being locked in.
3.   LIFFE imposes no limit on the number of T-bond options and futures positions an investor can hold.
4.   LIFFE provides an environment where short term and long term interest rate futures and options contracts trade simultaneously on one market floor – thus facilitating arbitrage opportunities such as that between Treasury bond futures and the Eurodollar interest rate future.

CHAPTER 14

Swaps

14.1 Introduction

One of the most rapidly growing and innovative areas in the international capital market has been the swap market. It is estimated to have grown from about $5 billion in 1982 to some $400 billion at the end of 1987.

The exponential growth in swaps is largely due to their flexibility. Swaps have become responsive vehicles for corporate treasurers, allowing almost instantaneous reactions to changing financial conditions. One of their most appealing features is that they can be 'fine-tuned' or 'customised' to fit almost any situation. Perhaps the ultimate attraction of swaps is that they improve profitability by facilitating the following:

- the obtaining of fixed rate financing at rates below those available by direct access to the public debt or private placement market;
- the accessing of fixed rate funding without tapping traditional sources of capital and thereby saving those sources for future use;
- the arrangement of long term floating rate debt at below market rates through selective use of an issuer's fixed rate capital market potential;
- the provision of alternative sources for floating rate funds when considering all possibilities in debt management;
- allowing the restructuring of the debt portfolio without raising new unnecessary finance;
- changing the composition of types of investment assets in line with portfolio management or interest rate views without involving sales or purchases.

A measure of acceptance and popularity was imparted to the swap technique by the historic Swiss franc/Deutschmark/US dollar currency swap between IBM and the World Bank in 1981. The interest rate swap developed as a means of exploiting interest rate differentials between the bond market and the short-term credit market.

Originally most swap transactions were matched deals in which an intermediary bank brought together two counterparties, or end-users with matching requirements. The intermediary bank would typically write separate contracts with the end-users, act as principal in both swap contracts, and charge an intermediation margin and possibly an arrangement fee.

The movement away from matched deals began in the dollar interest rate swap market, with banks developing techniques to enter into a swap agreement with one counterparty while taking out a temporary hedge in the bond or futures market until an offsetting swap was found. This process, known as 'warehousing', has been common in the dollar interest rate swap market since 1984. At the present time, a large number of financial intermediaries act as market-makers in this instrument. There are far less market-makers in interest rates swaps involving other currencies and even less in currency swaps.

14.2 Swap Structures

There are four basic structures, as follow, which encompass a definition of the most common type of swaps and which form the basic framework for more complex ones:

(a)   interest rate swaps;
(b)   basis swaps;
(c)   currency swaps;
(d)   fixed/fixed currency swaps.

14.3 Interest Rate Swaps

In terms of transaction volume the interest rate swap is by far the most common. Essentially it is a contract between two counterparties to exchange fixed interest rate payments (not principal). It normally involves two unrelated borrowers who have borrowed identical principal amounts for similar periods from different lenders, with one borrower paying a fixed rate and the other a floating rate of interest. The payment will be in the same currency on a given notional sum.

It allows a company or bank to convert existing assets or liabilities to another interest rate basis which reflects their current policy of financial management. Cost savings can arise from the pricing distinctions available to each party. Interest rate swaps can be utilised to convert floating rate debt into fixed rate debt, or vice versa. In addition, interest rate swaps can be executed on different floating rate measures if a market has enough floating rate alternatives. Generally, interest rate swaps are quoted as a fixed rate against a floating rate index in the particular currency being used.

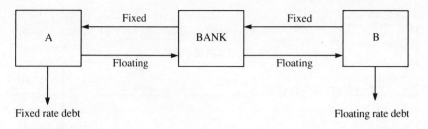

Figure 14.1   Interest rate swaps – interest rate flows

14.4   The Mechanics

The underlying concept in the swaps market is that each party has a different capability to access certain interest rate markets. Through exchange of each party's comparative edge, each party can obtain a better rate than through direct tapping of markets.

Stage One

Borrower A, a highly rated corporate name, has an excess of finely priced fixed rate debt. It would like to utilise this advantage to obtain lower cost floating rate interest on $20,000,000 of its debt. (It is assumed that A's next interest payment is in six months and is paid semi-annually in arrears).

Borrower B has a lower credit rating than A in the long-term debt markets, but has good access to short-term debt.

Stage Two

An intermediary arranges for Borrowers A and B to exchange their interest rate obligations at levels that produce a rate improvement for both of them. Every six months the following interest rate flows will occur (see Figure 14.1).

Stage Three

There is no need to exchange principal amount at either inception or maturity. As both flows are based on the same notional principal amount, the interest payments continue to be exchanged over the life of the agreement until final maturity.

The risk being assumed by the intermediary is contingent. If either party fails to make a swap payment to the intermediary, then the intermediary will not be obliged to make a payment to that party. Consequently, the risk

125

Swaps

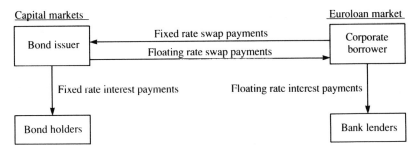

Figure 14.2 Basic logic of interest rate swaps

being carried by the intermediary in the event of default by one party is limited to the excess, if any, of interest payable to the other party over the interest to be received from that party.

14.5   Advantages of Interest Rate Swaps

By utilising each other's relative strengths in different markets, the swap counterparties can gain access to those markets at lower borrowing costs than could be otherwise achieved. For instance, a bond issuer can convert its fixed rate liability to floating rate while allowing a corporate borrower to convert the floating rate on its Euroloan to a fixed rate (see Figure 14.2). Underlying this basic logic of interest rate swaps are the large interest rate differentials which exist between the fixed and floating rate markets. For example, a borrowing of, say, seven years might lead to the differences in rates as shown in Table 14.1.

Strong credits can raise fixed rate funds in the capital markets at up to 3% per annum cheaper than the weaker credits and some entities will be too small or too weak even to gain access to the fixed rate markets. However, weaker credits usually have to pay no more than about $\frac{5}{8}$% per annum above that which strong credits pay in the Euroloan market for floating rate funds. Such interest rate differentials can be used to provide both parties with access to cheaper funds (see Figure 14.3), where the interest rate swap shows how the strong credit has converted its medium-long-term costs of borrowing from 11% per annum to the short-term interbank rate. Conversely, the weaker credit has been able to utilise an interest rate of $11\frac{7}{8}$% per annum for term funds, a rate of interest far cheaper than if it had issued bonds in its own name.

In the example cited, the bond issuer has not paid the corporate borrowers $\frac{7}{8}$% per annum margin over LIBOR. It has, therefore, assumed only part of the corporate's floating rate interest liability. The 'partial swap'

126

Table 14.1. Sample borrowing rates for seven years funds

	Capital markets (fixed rates)	Euroloan market (floating rates)
Strong credits (e.g. major banks)	Lowest rates	LIBOR $+\frac{3}{8}\%$ p.a.
Weaker credits (e.g. medium sized corporates)	Up to 3% p.a. higher	libor $+1\%$ p.a.
Differential	3%	$\frac{5}{8}\%$

element is used to balance the advantage for each counterparty and is usually negotiable in arranging an interest rate swap.

If the fixed rate swap payment has been $11\frac{1}{4}\%$ per annum the bond issuer would have retained $\frac{1}{4}\%$ from the fixed payment flows and effectively obtained funds at LIBOR minus $\frac{1}{4}\%$ per annum, while the corporate borrower would have converted its borrowing cost to $12\frac{1}{8}\%$ per annum fixed ($11\frac{1}{4}\% + \frac{7}{8}\%$). In addition to locking into a fixed interest rate, it is usual for the fixed rate payer to reimburse the bond issuer with the issue costs. This is because the weaker credit is indirectly gaining access to the fixed rate capital markets through the swap arrangement.

14.6 Variation on Interest Rate Swaps

Suppose a corporate borrower wishes to have fixed rate funds but does not want to enter into a swap. By acting as a lender and an intermediary, the bank can raise floating rate funds and through an interest rate swap with a counterparty (e.g. a bond issuer) convert its funding cost to a fixed rate and onlend to the corporate borrower on this basis (Figure 14.4).

Another variation (Figure 14.5) arises when there is only one counterparty which seeks to convert its fixed rate liability to a floating rate but does not want to borrow new funds. By purchasing fixed rate bonds in the

Figure 14.3 Interest rate differentials in an interest rate swap

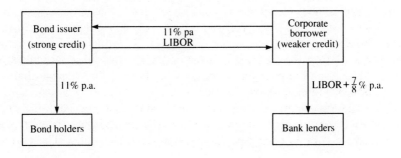

Swaps

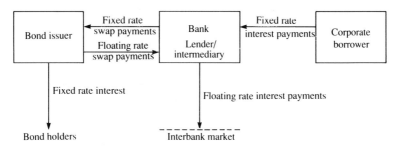

Figure 14.4   Access to fixed rate funds without entering into a swap

market (or matching against an existing holding), fixed rate interest income can be generated and then swapped for floating rate income and so match the bank's funding liability to the interbank market. If the bonds are priced at more than par, the premium could be recouped by charging the customer an arrangement fee. If the bonds are priced at a discount, this discount could be booked as a front end fee to the bank, without charging the customer. This structure can be useful for smaller swaps if suitable bonds are available in the right size and at the right price.

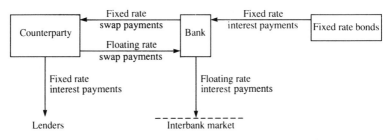

Figure 14.5   Conversion of fixed rate liability into floating rate without accessing new funds

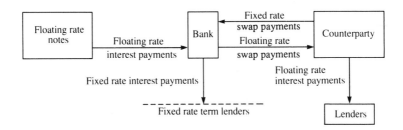

Figure 14.6   Conversion of floating rate liability into fixed rate without accessing new funds

Similarly a bank can assist a sole counterparty which seeks to convert its floating rate liability to a fixed rate but does not wish to borrow new funds (Figure 14.6). By purchasing floating rate notes in the market (or matching against an existing holding) the bank can generate floating rate interest to exchange for fixed rate income and match the fixed rate funding liability. Floating rate notes are usually available at a small discount which could be treated as a front end fee. This structure is useful for smaller swaps mainly.

14.7 Basis Swaps

The structure of the basis rate swap is the same as the straight interest rate swap, with the exception that floating interest calculated on one basis is exchanged for floating interest calculated on a different basis. The forerunner of this type of swap was the US dollar prime rate for LIBOR swap. Subsequently larger markets developed for the exchange of one month US dollar LIBOR for six month US dollar LIBOR and more recently US dollar LIBOR for US dollar commercial paper. The availability of the basis rate swap market provides an excellent facility to arbitrage spreads between different floating rate funding sources. More importantly, it provides a discrete and most efficient method for Europeans, in particular, to simulate the US commercial paper funding market without the necessity of meeting the stringent US requirements for a commercial paper programme.

14.8 Currency Swaps

A currency swap is a legal arrangement to exchange payments denominated in one currency for those denominated in another, typically for a period of between two and ten years. The market generally operates on the standard of the fixed rate of the foreign currency against six months US LIBOR, although it is possible to have currency swaps structured differently. The exchange rate is set at the beginning of the transaction and is fixed for the entire life. There must be an exchange of the principal amounts at the final maturity.

The term 'currency swap' sometimes gives rise to confusion as it has two meanings. In the foreign exchange markets, the term 'swap' is used to denote a spot sale and forward purchase of a currency (Chapter one). In the capital markets a swap usually involves an exchange of interest payments and principal denominated in one currency for payments in another. It is with the latter that we are concerned in this section. There are two main types of currency swap: fixed/fixed currency swaps and fixed/floating currency swaps. The latter are usually known as 'cross currency' interest rate swaps.

129

14.9 Fixed/Fixed Currency Swaps

Fixed interest payments in one currency are exchanged for fixed interest payments in another. The following three basic stages are common to all currency swaps.

Stage One:

Initial exchange of principal: at the commencement of the swap, the counterparties exchange the principal amounts of the swap at an agreed rate of exchange. Although this rate is usually based on the spot exchange rate, using the mid-rate, a forward rate set in advance of the swap commencement date can also be used. The initial exchange may either be on a 'notional' basis (i.e. no physical exchange of principal amounts) or a 'physical' exchange basis. The standard transaction size is usually $US5,000,000.

Stage Two

Ongoing exchanges of interest: once the principal amounts are established, the counterparties exchange interest payments based on the outstanding principal amounts, at the respective fixed interest rates agreed at the outset of the transaction.

Stage Three

Re-exchange of principal amounts: on the maturity date, the counterparties re-exchange the principal amounts established at the outset. It is important to note that this re-exchange on maturity, is conducted for the same amount and, therefore, at the same exchange rate as the initial exchange, irrespective of whether such initial exchange is a physical exchange or not. This three stage process is standard practice in the swap market and results in debt raised in one currency being transferred into a fully hedged fixed rate liability in another.

For example, suppose borrower A prefers his or her obligations to be in floating rate $US but can obtain preferential rates relative to borrower B by tapping the Swiss franc market. Borrower B, on the other hand, prefers obligations to be in fixed rate SFs, but can obtain preferential terms relative to Borrower A by borrowing in the floating rate $US market.

Borrower A will, therefore, borrow in the fixed rate Swiss franc market and borrower B will borrow in the floating rate $US market. A will then pay the proceeds of his or her SF loan, via an intermediary, to borrower B and vice-versa, B will pay the proceeds of his or her $US loan, via the intermediary,

Figure 14.7 Stage one in a currency swap

to borrower A. As shown in Figure 14.7, borrower A then has access to $US and borrower B access to Swiss francs.

Figure 14.8 shows that at each interest payment date, the borrowers will pay to the intermediary, an amount of currency based on the agreed interest rate ($US flow will be typically based on six month LIBOR and the SF flow

Figure 14.8 Stage two in a currency swap

on the fixed rate agreed at the commencement of the swap). At maturity the original principal amounts are re-exchanged through the intermediary as indicated in Figure 14.9. Clearly, this example can be applied to both existing and new debt, plus obligations that have been arranged through a capital market issue. Investment assets can also be swapped into another currency using this facility.

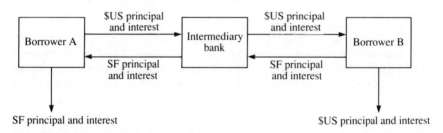

Figure 14.9 Stage three in a currency swap

14.10 Currency Coupon Swaps

One of the most important features of the swap market is that swaps enable a borrower to raise funds in the market to which it has best access but to make interest and principal payments in its preferred form of currency. This separation of the funding decision and the choice of servicing debt enables borrowers to exploit their comparative advantages.

131

Swaps

Currency coupon swaps are essentially combinations of fixed rate currency swaps and interest rate swaps. The structure of the transaction is identical to that of a fixed/fixed currency swap except that fixed rate interest in one currency is exchanged for floating rate interest in another currency.

14.11 Asset Swaps

Traditionally swaps were used to transform the currency or interest base of liabilities. Over the past few years, the same techniques have increasingly been used to transform assets. Asset swaps (or synthetic securities as they are also known) simply combine an asset and a swap. A fixed rate asset can, therefore, be transferred into a floating rate asset either in the same or a different currency. The market works by taking advantage of price imperfections in the bond and swap market. The technique is to buy bonds relatively inexpensively in relationship to credit rating, by trading in the secondary market and to combine them with an interest rate swap.

The bulk of the market has involved the creation of synthetic floating rate notes (FRNs). The buyers of synthetic assets include commercial banks seeking high yielding assets, FRN portfolio managers, and corporate and institutional fund managers. Buyers may either purchase bonds and arrange separate swaps themselves, or buy a package of bonds and a swap from an intermediary. Intermediaries tend to be major investment banks, merchant banks or commercial banks with a presence in the secondary bond market, with proven swap and marketing/sales capabilities.

14.12 Swap Risks

Risks typically associated with swap activities largely relate to the roles of individual parties in the swap. A broker, for instance, incurs no risk once he has received the fee for bringing the two counterparties together. Conversely, a principal, an end-user, or an intermediary, incur a greater variety of risks over a much longer period.

Credit Risk

Swaps are not just an interest rate play; they are a bet on the continued creditworthiness of the counterparty, i.e. the risk that the counterparty may default. Approximately, six companies with single A credit ratings have gone bankrupt in the last decade. Many more have slid from single A rating (or better) to below investment grade. Fortunately, however, an exposure is not a liability unless there is a default. Even then, it is not the principal or notional amount that is at risk but the replacement cost of a missing interest rate stream.

The amount of money involved in credit risk can be particularly large. For example, take a typical swap: a $100,000,000 seven year transaction with five-and-a-half years to maturity. Suppose the bank commenced its floating payments at 11% but then interest rates subsequently reduced by 300 basis points. The borrower continues to pay fixed rates at $11\frac{1}{2}\%$. Marking the swap to market, the bank calculates its exposure as 17.8% or $17,800,000. That is how much it would cost to replace the original stream of payments. The problem, of course, is that nobody is going to come up with $11\frac{1}{2}\%$, i.e., the original fixed-rate payment, in the lower-rate environment.

Position Risk

Position risk is the risk that interest rates and exchanges rates will move adversely, after the deal is struck. Losses can arise either if interest rates and exchange rates move adversely resulting in a position loss, or if interest rates move favourably, resulting in a position gain but with the counterparty defaulting.

There are three main features of position risk, as follows:

1. Position risk varies over the life of a deal according to movements in interest rates and/or exchange rates.
2. Position risk can be either positive or negative.
3. Position risk cannot be determined in advance.

14.13 Quantification of the Risk

Most players in the swap market take account of several factors in assessing risk. Risk is then quantified by aggregating the following components:

1. *Interest Differential Formula*

$$P \times \frac{D}{100} \times T$$

where

P = the principal amount of the swap

D = the difference between the fixed rate applicable to one leg of the swap and the estimate of the maximum/minimum rates applicable to the floating rate leg of the swap during its term. These two differentials (i.e. between the fixed rate and the maximum floating rate and between the fixed rate and the minimum floating rate) are separately applied to the above formula in order to arrive at individually assessed risks for

133

each counterparty (as the risks cannot both materialise, they should not be aggregated).

T = the remaining term of the swap in years.

2. Settlement Risk

An amount equating to 10% of the exposure arrived at under the above formula is added if a settlement risk on the gross interest cash flow arises. This does not always apply since swaps are settled net.

3. Internal Assessment Rate

A percentage is applied to the quantified interest rate risk to arrive at the assessed exposure for internal purposes. To realise the maximum risk would require both an immediate default by one of the parties and an interest rate differential at the maximum figure for each year during the life of the transaction. The interest rate risk reduces over the life of the swap to zero at maturity.

4. Foreign Exchange Risk

An amount equating to approximately 15% of the principal amount being swapped is added if there is more than one currency involved and accordingly a forward foreign exchange risk exists. This assessment is not reduced over the life of the swap as exchange rate movements can be volatile at all times.

14.14 Advantages to the Bank

Off balance sheet

(a) By arranging swaps and acting as the intermediary, a bank can earn substantial fee income without utilising any assets. Interest rate swaps could provide a major source of off balance sheet income in the future.

(b) Arrangement fees usually amount to between $\frac{1}{4}$% and $\frac{1}{2}$% flat, while the intermediary fees range from about 0.1% pa to 0.375% pa (depending on risk) during the life of the swap. In both cases these payments are calculated on the principal sum involved in the swap transaction, while the risk to the bank is only a small fraction of this figure. The return to the bank is, therefore, enhanced considerably.

On balance sheet

(c)   In marketing to a wide range of corporate customers, a bank can use interest rate swaps to offer term lending at fixed rates of interest in major currencies.

(d)   By providing fixed rate term loans, the bank is assured of 100% utilisation of its commitments with resultant increased margin income compared with partially used lines.

14.15   Background on the US dollar Swap Market

The liquidity and depth of the dollar interest rate swap market owes much to the ease of hedging swaps in the US Treasury bond repo (see Section 14.17) or futures market and does much to explain why growth in the interest rate swap market has outstripped growth in the currency swap market. The principal amount of outstanding currency swap contracts is estimated to have increased from $2–3 billion in 1982 to perhaps $80–100 billion by the end of 1987, while the aggregate notional principal of outstanding interest rate swaps rose from a similar base in 1982 to an estimated $350 billion at the end of 1987. Liquidity in the interest rate swap market has been further aided by the moves towards a standardised product. In mid-1985 both the International Swap Dealers Association (ISDA) and the British Bankers' Association brought out standardised dealing terms and documentation for interest rate swaps.

14.16   Pricing of Interest Rate Swaps

The ultimate determinants of the price of an interest rate swap are the supply and demand for fixed and floating rate finance. Specifically, the swap price is closely related to yields on government securities and Eurobonds. Yields in the Eurobond market are important since the basic interest rate swap is essentially an arbitrage between this market and the market for short-term credit. Government securities, particularly US Treasuries, are important as the primary hedging instrument for interest rate swaps. To the extent that the price of a swap is the cost of producing it from the warehouse, the influence of government securities (both cash and futures) will dominate Eurobond yield considerations.

In the dollar swap market, the swap price is quoted on a semi-annual bond basis as a spread over the US Treasury bond of corresponding maturity, in relation to a given floating rate, usually six month LIBOR. A swap rate of 55/50 for a five year swap, for example, means that the fixed interest payable in return for receiving six month dollar LIBOR is 55 basis

135

Swaps

points above the equivalent US Treasury rate. Similarly the fixed rate receivable under the opposite swap is 50 basis points above the Treasury rate. Example 14.1 shows the process for calculating a five year US dollar interest rate swap price for a counterparty with reference to market rates.

Example 14.1 Pricing a five year US dollar interest rate swap

Step One
Obtain US Treasury price from the dealers. Suppose that the Treasury $8\frac{3}{8}\%$ due November 1994 is currently quoted 97.17 bid and 97.19 offered. To calculate the fixed rate the bank pays for five years we take the offered price.

Step Two
Determine yield to maturity from this price (e.g. from yield sheet) Suppose this gives 8.955%.

Step Three
Suppose the five year Treasury spread is 88/80. This means that the fixed interest payable to the market maker in return for receiving six month dollar LIBOR is 88 basis points above the equivalent US Treasury rate. The spreads will move daily, but for dollar swaps they are reasonably stable.

Step Four
The price of the Treasury will depend upon whether you pay or receive the fixed rate on the swap. For example, Treasury quote is 19.17/19. We can sell the Treasury at 97.17 or buy it at 97.19. We are looking to pay fixed rate, as in Figure 14.10. Therefore we buy the Treasury at 97.19 giving a yield of 8.955%. As the bank is paying fixed, they will pay the low spread, i.e. 80 basis points.

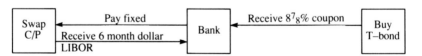

Figure 14.10 Pricing interest rate swaps

Step Five
This is then priced on an annual basis. So: effective yield + spread = 8.955 + 0.80 = 9.755% for a semi-annual bond

For an annual bond, the rate is:

$$\left[1 + \frac{0.09755}{2} \right]^2 - 1 = 9.9929\%$$

Hedging swaps using repurchase agreements

Step Six

This rate is then converted from an actual days basis onto a 360 day money market basis:

$$9.9929 \times \frac{360}{365} = 9.856\%$$

Therefore, we pay 9.85% per annum for five years.

Let us now consider the effect of a change in US interest rates.

Falling interest rates

A decrease in interest rates means that the counterparty pays the bank less, e.g. 9.8%. However, as yields fall, so bond prices increase and the Treasury held by the bank would increase in price. If that is perfectly hedged they will make the five basis points they lose in absolute rate (9.85 − 9.80) plus the eight basis point spread on the swap price, less the $\frac{2}{32}$ or so spread on buying/selling the T-bond. This is usually one basis point per year, discounted up front. For a $10,000,000 transaction for five years at 9.85%, this gives brokerage = $3,840.

Rising interest rates

The bank will protect itself from rising interest rates because when the swap position is covered, they will be paying six month LIBOR. This is done through the use of Eurodollar futures contracts.

As rates rise, the price of three month Eurodollar futures will fall. The bank will profit from this by selling the future now and buying it back at a later date. The number of contracts required for the hedge is calculated as follows:

$$\text{No. of contracts} = \frac{\text{Swap value} \times \dfrac{6 \text{ month LIBOR}}{3 \text{ month futures}}}{\text{Nominal value of futures}}$$

$$= \frac{10,000,000 \times 6/3}{1,000,000} = 20 \text{ contracts}$$

If dollar LIBOR increases by $\frac{1}{2}$%, then the futures fall 50 basis points. This gives a profit from the futures position of:

$20 \times 50 \times \$25$ (tick size) = $25,000 gain

14.17 Hedging Swaps Using Repurchase (Repo) Agreements

As an alternative to buying the Treasury bond outright, the bank could enter into a repurchase agreement. This arrangement is made through a primary Treasury bond dealer. By putting the bond on repo, the bank does

Swaps

Figure 14.11 A repurchase (repo) agreement

not pay for it, but is effectively lent the money. For this service they pay a fee which is market determined. At the time of writing it was around $6-6\frac{1}{2}\%$. When the position is closed, it is repriced to the market and the account settled (see Figure 14.11). In the example given in Figure 14.11, the bank will make a 'pick-up' of $(1.6625 - 1.475) = 19$ basis points from the repurchase agreement.

Example 14.2 Reverse Repos
If the bank is short the T-bond (i.e. a receiver of fixed and payer of floating interest) then it will pay the coupon and receive the 'reverse repo' rate (see Figure 14.12). With this arrangement the bank will lose $(1.575 - 2.0625) = 49$ basis points which could prove costly if held too long.

These arrangements are typically made through primary T-bond dealers and are usually only available to major financial institutions.

Figure 14.12 A reverse repo agreement

14.18 Secondary Swap Market

Although the interest rate swap market has moved further than the currency swap market away from the matched deal towards a tradeable instrument, the process is far from complete. The secondary market remains extremely thin because of the mutuality of obligations involved in a swap. It also usually involves large cash flows to pay out the swap.

Suppose US dollar LIBOR is 10% and the swap has a further three years to maturity, the purchaser would need to pay $2\% \times$ principal/year, discounted to its present value. For a $10,000,000 transaction, with a 2% differential in the receiving and paying rates and a 10% discount rate, the payout would be approximately $500,000.

These transactions tend to be quite complex due to the legal issues and documentation involved. They have been increasingly used to dump swaps where limits are reached or capital tied up, in an endeavour to introduce more profitable business.

138

14.19   Eurobond Issues with Attached Currency Swaps

The advantages of these issues depend on the favourability of market conditions. One of the fastest growing sectors in recent years was in issues of Euro-Australian dollar and Euro New Zealand dollar bonds with attached currency swaps. They increased from about $150 million in 1984 to $2,800 million in 1986. In simple terms the swap exploits the differential between interest rates in the domestic markets and the Euromarkets. The Australian and New Zealand domestic bond markets are poorly developed and the supply of fixed rate funds from the banking sector is limited. This has produced a large pool of companies in search of fixed rate liabilities. In Australia, an additional oddity was provided by the fact that several Australian companies had earlier borrowed through US dollar syndicated credits and, therefore, acquired a high currency exposure in US dollars.

The pricing of these issues is an interesting process, an example of which is given below.

Example 14.3 Pricing the swap side of a Eurobond Issue

Suppose an Australian company issue an Australian Eurobond with the following details:

Amount AUD 100m
Coupon 14%
Issue Price $101\frac{1}{2}$
Fees $1\frac{1}{2}$ (co-managers)
Maturity 3 years
Expenses $A150,000 (legal expenses, printing, etc.)

They also enter a swap arrangement with a bank, to receive the AUD coupon and pay USD six month LIBOR less a certain number of basis points. How does the bank calculate this rate? Figure 14.13 shows how the bank would arrange its payments and receipts for this exercise.

Step One
Calculate the internal rate of return for the Eurobond. The IRR or yield to maturity is the rate which sets the present value of the interest income stream and principal equal to the market price of the bond, and is given by the following equation:

$$MP = \sum_{j=1}^{mn} \left[\frac{I/M}{(1 + (r/m)^j)} \right] + \frac{P}{(1 + (r/m)^{mn})}$$

where
I = interest payment per $1,000 per annum
M = number of interest payments per annum

139

Swaps

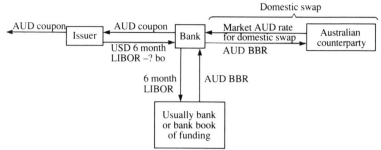

Note: AUD BBR = Australian dollar bank bill rate

Figure 14.13 Eurobond issue with attached currency swap

n = number of years to maturity
P = principle value
MP = market price per \$1,000
r = internal rate of return

This equation cannot be solved algebraically – rather it involves an iterative process. In this example the IRR is calculated to be 14.0646%

Step Two
Suppose the swap rate for fixed rate AUD/USD LIBOR = 14.60%. The difference between swap rate and IRR = 53.5 basis points. As this relates to AUD, we need to convert to USD. We have assumed a conversion rate of 1.2 (from calculation using forward AUD FX rates).

Thus $\dfrac{53.5}{1.2}$ = 45 basis points under LIBOR

The cash flows in this situation, given that the AUD/USD rate = 0.73, are shown in Figures 14.14 and 14.15. The difference between the amount the

Figure 14.14 Pricing the swap side of a Eurobond issue – the initial cash flow

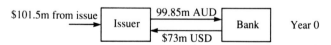

Figure 14.15 Pricing the swap side of a Eurobond issue – cash flow on maturity

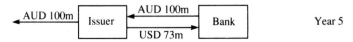

issuer receives and the amount he pays the bank is due to the expenses of the issue:

$101\frac{1}{4}$ (issue price $- 1\frac{1}{2}$ (fees) $- 0.15$ (expenses) $= 99.85\%$ of $100,000,000 = $99.85,000,000

The exchange rate set initially is fixed for the whole period.

AUD Eurobond issues are 95% swap driven although recent market conditions have been unfavourable, resulting in a fall in the number of issues. However, there has been a rise in the number of New Zealand dollar and Canadian dollar issues, which have swaps and high coupons relative to USD, Deutschmark, sterling, Swiss francs, etc.

14.20 Variations on the Swap

(a) Zero Coupon Swaps

A zero coupon swap is similar to the conventional swap structure. However, whereas one party makes regular periodic floating rate payments, the other party makes only one fixed rate payment on the scheduled termination of the agreement. The fixed payment is structured to reflect the compounding of all fixed swap payments which would normally be made during the life of a conventional interest rate swap (see Figure 14.16).

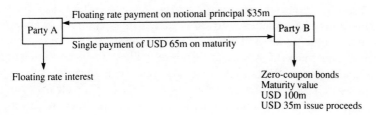

Figure 14.16 Zero coupon swap

(b) Forward Swaps

A forward swap is an obligation to enter a swap at some time in the future at a predetermined rate. If current rates appear favourable the borrower can use forward swaps to eliminate any uncertainty over rate movements until swap commencement.

(c)   Amortising Swaps

In an amortising swap agreement, the notional principal amount amortises over the life of the swap. This type of structure is used when the underlying borrowing being hedged amortises over time.

14.21   Conclusion

The attraction of swaps are numerous, but the two most important factors are:

1. the exploitation of arbitrage opportunities to lower significantly the costs of funds; and
2. the ability actively to manage assets and liabilities using both hedging and trading strategies.

Swaps may be used to hedge existing positions, although the use of swaps for hedging is less related to the imperfection of markets than to the volatility of markets.

In a sense, swaps also extend existing markets. Currency swaps extend the forward exchange market beyond what is usually available, while interest rate swaps effectively extend the market in interest rate futures beyond their current eighteen months limit into the medium term.

Swaps will be a permanent feature of the financial landscape, although the exponential growth seen in recent years is unlikely to continue. In response to the decline in profit margins caused by increased competition, there may be a tendency towards increasingly complex swaps related to more exotic underlying instruments and the spread of the swap technique into new markets. A second response is likely to be continued efforts to standardise products and move towards the tradeability of swaps, with possibly a swap futures contract or some type of 'swap clearing house' with which swap dealers could write contracts and net their positions.

Appendix 1 Pricing model for a European call option

$$P = e^{-rt} [FN(d_1) - EN(d_2)]$$
where
$$d_1 = [1n(F/E) + \tfrac{1}{2}\sigma 2_t]/6t$$
and
$$d_2 = d_1 - \sigma\sqrt{t}$$

where

F = current forward outright price for the expiration date
E = exercise price (strike price)
σ = standard deviation of continuously compounded rate of change in spot price (volatility)
t = time to expiration in years
r = interbank deposit rate for base currency for the period of the option
N = cumulative normal probability distribution for bracketed values d_1 and d_2 i.e. probability that a deviation less than d will occur in a normal distribution with a mean of zero and a standard deviation of 1.

Note: derived from Garman, Mark B, and Kohlhagen, Steven W., 'Foreign currency option values', *Journal of International Money and Finance*, December 1983, pp. 231–7.

Appendix 2 Arithmetic formula for the delta on a currency call option

$$e^{-i_f t} \, \Phi \left[\frac{\ln(S_p/E_p) + (i_d - i_f)}{v \sqrt{t}} + \tfrac{1}{2} v \sqrt{t} \right]$$

where

S_p = spot rate
E_p = exercise price
i_d = domestic interest rate
i_f = foreign interest rate
v = volatility
t = time to expiration

Bibliography

Atkinson, B. (1988), 'Financial instruments – Interest and currency management', *Tolley's Tax Planning*, Tolley, London, pp. 279–303.

Back, P. (1989), 'Developing sound relationships', *Banking World*, February, p. 51.

Bank for International Settlements (1986), *Recent Innovations in International Banking*, Study Group Report.

Bank of England Quarterly Bulletin (1986), 'Recent trends in real interest rates', September, pp. 359–63.

Bank of England Quarterly Bulletin (1987), 'Recent developments in the swap market', February, pp. 66–79.

Banker, The (1988), 'Interest rate and currency swaps', July, p. 15.

Banker, The (1988), 'Capped floating rate notes', May, p. 64.

Banking World (1985), 'Cry of the corporate treasurer', March, pp. 24–5.

Banking World (1988), 'Futures and options – survey', April, pp. 50-5.

Banking World (1986), 'Financial futures – special account', July, pp. 32–7.

Bookstaber, R. M. (1987), *Option Pricing and Investment Strategies*, Probus, Chicago.

Buckley, A. (1986), *Multinational Finance*, Phillip Allan, Oxford.

Business International Corporation (1987), *Managing Risks and Costs Through Financial Innovations*, Economist Publications, London.

Carrington, M. L. (1987), 'Interest rate risk-managing exposure', *London Accountant*, Summer, pp. 11-12.

Chamberlain, G. (1987), *Trading in Options*, second edition, Woodhead-Faulkner, Cambridge.

Chew, L. (1988), 'Currency volatility on the boil again', *Risk*, vol. 1, no. 2, January.

Coats, A. (1987), 'A case study on interest rate risk management', *The Treasurer*, November, pp. 57–9.

Coopers & Lybrand (1987), *A Guide to Financial Instruments*, Euromoney Publications, London.

Coward, M. and Thomas, L. 'When average can be good', *Risk*, vol. 1, no. 8, July, pp. 43–4.

Bibliography

Cox, J. C. and Rubinstein, M. (1985), *Option Markets*, Prentice Hall, Hemel Hempstead.

D'Souza, F. (1987), 'Swaps new moves', Supplement to *Euromoney and Corporate Finance*, July, pp. 30–3.

Dwyer, M. (1988), 'Futures and options – a valuable asset management tool', *CBSI Journal*, March, pp. 17–19.

Ernst & Whinney (1986), *Currency Options*, April.

Euromoney Corporate Finance Supplement (1986), '1st, 2nd, 3rd Generation Risk Management', *Euromoney*, September, pp. 24–51.

Euromoney (1986), *Swap Finance*, Euromoney Publications, London.

Euromoney Corporate Finance Supplement (1987), 'Risk Running', *Euromoney*, July.

Euromoney (1987), 'Who's top in swaps?', January, pp. 25–9.

Euromoney (1988), 'Why do we need financial engineering?', September, pp. 190–200.

Euromoney (1985), 'Interest rate caps and collars', Euromoney Special Supplement, December.

Euromoney (1987), Shearson Lehman Brothers, 'Guide to debt management', Sponsored Supplement to *Euromoney*, April.

Evans, G. (1986), 'Why new products come and go', Euromoney Special Survey, pp. 2–8.

Fall, W. (1987), 'Documentation issues on interest rate swaps and forward rate agreements', *The Treasurer*, November, pp. 45–9.

Fall, W. (1988), 'Caps vs swaps vs hybrids', *Risk*, vol. 1, no. 5, April, pp. 21–4.

First Interstate (1987), 'Financial tools for managing risk', Supplement to *Euromoney*, August.

Fitzgerald, M. D. (1983), *Financial Futures*, Euromoney Publications, London.

Fitzgerald, M. D. (1986), *Financial Options*, Euromoney Publications, London.

Futures and Options World (1988), 'Do banks cash in on corporate Angst?', *Futures and Options World*, August, pp. 33–7.

Gardener, E. P. M. (1987) 'Interest rate risk and the banking firm', *Interest Margin Analysis Revisited*, Institute of European Finance Monograph No. 4.

Gatheral, J. (1987), 'Managing interest rate volatility', *Arab Banker*, March/April, pp. 22–3.

Gilbart Lectures (1987), *New Financial Instruments*, The Chartered Institute of Bankers, London.

Glaum, M. (1988), 'The foreign exchange risk management of UK multinational corporations and their attitudes towards financial innovation: an empirical study', LUT Working Paper No. 185.

Bibliography

Glaum, M. (1988), 'The management of foreign exchange risk in multinational corporations', LUBC Monograph No. 4.

Goode, T. (1987), 'A review of interest rate risk management techniques', *The Treasurer*, November, pp. 49–51.

Grumball, C. (1987), *Managing Interest Rate Risk*, Woodhead-Faulkner, Cambridge.

Heywood, J. (1987), 'Interest rate risk in banks', *The Treasurer*, November, pp. 53–6.

Hislop, A. (1987), 'A model approach', *The Banker*, August, pp. 15–17.

Hodson, D. (1987), *Corporate Finance and Treasury Management*, Gee & Co.

Isaac, G. (1985), 'Interest rate swaps', *The Treasurer*, October, pp. 17–21.

Kenyon, A. (1981), *Currency Risk Management*, Wiley, New York.

Labuszewski, J. W. and Nyhoff, J. (1988), *Trading Financial Futures: Markets, Methods, Strategies and Tactics*, Wiley, New York.

Langdon, L. M. (1988), 'Hedging against changing interest rates', *The Bankers' Magazine*, July/August, pp. 39–43.

MacDougall, R. (1988), 'Switch or shrink', *The Banker*, March, pp. 23–8.

Mand, S. S. (1988), 'Swaptions – pricing and hedging', University of London.

McMahon, R.J. (1988), 'Understanding interest rate swaps', *The Bankers' Magazine*, September/October, pp. 59–62.

Miller, M. (1986), 'Financial innovation: the last 20 years and the next', University of Chicago Working Paper.

Redhead, K. and Hughes, S. (1988), *Financial Risk Management*, Gower, Cambridge.

Risk (1987), 'Collaring an option with a cap that fits', vol. 1, no. 1, December, pp. 18–19.

Robinson, N. (1988), 'Toy-town time in the markets', *The Banker*, May, pp. 56–8.

Ross, D. and Clark, I. (1987), *International Treasury Management*, Woodhead-Faulkner, Cambridge.

Ross, D. R. (1988), 'Interest rate swaps', *The Treasurer*, March, pp. 25–9.

Schall, L. D. and Haley, W. H. (1986), *Introduction to Financial Management*, McGraw Hill, New York.

Scott, P. N. (1985), 'Interest rate options, guarantees and caps', *The Treasurer*, October, pp. 29–31.

Shapiro, A. C. (1986), *Multinational Financial Management*, second edition, Allyn & Bacon, London.

Shreeve, G. and McDougal, R. N. (1987), 'Quality not quantity', *The Banker*, August, pp. 12–15.

Smart, E. (1988), 'The banks and risk management', Cambridge Seminar, *Banking World*, November, pp. 74–5.

Bibliography

Stillit, D. (1987), 'Swap finance', Supplement to *Euromoney and Corporate Finance*, June, pp. 20–1.

Sutton, W. H. (1988), *The Currency Options Handbook*, Woodhead-Faulkner, Cambridge.

Tiner, J. and Conneely, J. (1987), *Accounting for Treasury Products: A practical guide to accounting, tax and risk control*, Woodhead-Faulkner, Cambridge.

Trèves, D. (1984), 'The case for the FRA', *Euromoney*, November, p. 196.

Von Pfeil, E. (1988), *Effective Control of Currency Risks*, St Martins Press.

Walmsley, J. (1988), *The New Financial Instruments – An Investors Guide*, Wiley, New York.

Watson, A. and Altringham, R. (1985), '*Treasury management - international banking operations*', The Chartered Institute of Bankers, London.

Weisweiller, R. (ed.) (1986), *Arbitrage: Opportunities and techniques in the financial and commodity markets*, Woodhead-Faulkner, Cambridge.

Wilson, N. (1988), 'Safe at last', *Risk*, vol. 1, no. 8, July, p. 5.

Wisbey, J. (1988), 'Hedging interest rate exposure', *Risk*, vol. 1, no. 7, June.

Index

Index

Index